Montaigne's Discovery of Man

Montaigne's Discovery of Man

THE HUMANIZATION OF A HUMANIST

by

Donald M. Frame

GREENWOOD PRESS, PUBLISHERS
WESTPORT, CONNECTICUT

Library of Congress Cataloging in Publication Data

Frame, Donald Murdoch, 1911-
Montaigne's discovery of man.

Reprint. Originally published: New York : Columbia University Press, 1955.
1. Montaigne, Michel de, 1533-1592--Criticism and interpretation. 2. Humanism. I. Title.
PQ1643.F72 1983 844'.3 83-12716
ISBN 0-313-24120-1 (lib. bdg.)

A Guggenheim Fellowship and a Fulbright Grant enabled me to complete this book. It is a pleasure to record my gratitude.

D. M. F.

Reprinted in 1983 by Greenwood Press
A division of Congressional Information Service, Inc.
88 Post Road West, Westport, Connecticut 06881

Printed in the United States of America

P

TO KITTY

parce que c'est elle

Contents

Montaigne's Discovery of Man

Introduction

THE UNFOLDING OF MONTAIGNE'S THOUGHT

MOST of Montaigne's remarks about the common herd (*le vulgaire*) are not flattering. It would be amazing if they were. The great ancients whom he loved almost from the cradle, his favorite moderns who imbibed the ancient wisdom as he did and used it in translation like Amyot, in poetry like Ronsard, or in action like La Boétie, held that the common herd was to be led with blinkers, if not hated and thrust aside as a thing profane. Their undemocratic contempt was not so much social as intellectual; they shunned not the poor but the ignorant. Though they agreed with Rabelais that the study of ancient letters had at last led France out of the darkness of centuries smelling of the "infelicity and calamity of the Goths," they felt that not all Frenchmen had emerged. Only the humanists, those who had the will and the way to devote themselves to the *litterae humaniores,* had made the climb from the shadows and firelight of the cave into the brilliant sunlight of the French Renaissance.

For all his love of freedom, simplicity, and naturalness, Montaigne started his quest of happiness and wisdom as a humanist. Thus it is not surprising to find, among his milder remarks about *le vulgaire* in the early essays, one to the effect that we would be foolish to believe all that we cannot disprove, for, if we did, the belief of the common herd would be as mobile as a weathercock.

What is surprising is a very short addition to this passage, one of hundreds that Montaigne made in the last years of his life.

Right after *le vulgaire* he added: *et nous sommes tous du vulgaire* —"and we are all of the common herd." This statement might be banal today, but it was pretty radical and unhumanistic for a learned writer in 1590. And it is central to many of the changes in Montaigne's thinking which are the subject of this book.

The best book about Montaigne was written long ago by Montaigne himself. In it he warned the thousands of us who are still talking about him to beware. "I would willingly come back from the other world," he tells us, "to give the lie to any man who portrayed me other than I was, even if it were to honor me."

For him, to be known was the essence of life; to be misunderstood, a sort of death. Knowing that interpretation inevitably involves distortion and that man's complex and contradictory nature must be studied long and hard to be judged aright, he wished that fewer people would meddle in this "high and hazardous enterprise." As for himself, he felt that in twenty years and three books of essays he had covered the ground pretty thoroughly. "If you look around," he says, "you will find that I have said everything or suggested everything. . . . I leave nothing about me to be desired or guessed."

But although he has told us much, he has in fact left much to be guessed. His respect for facts and his awareness of variation lead him to observe but rarely to generalize; and one of his few generalizations about himself is that a whole swarm of conflicting epithets seem to fit him equally well.

Perhaps indeed it is even more *because* he tells so much that he leaves us guessing; for the more he tells, the more he contradicts—or seems to contradict—himself. Critics of three centuries pronounced him either devious or inconsistent, mainly because they lacked the critical apparatus to study chronologically a book that is professedly a record of change. Painstaking scholarship, especially in the last fifty years, has greatly narrowed the area of misunderstanding and difference of opinion. Yet even today a good case can be made by a man of the stature of Gide for an unbelieving Montaigne, and an equally good case at the opposite extreme for Montaigne as a faithful medieval theologian. Some of the wide divergences are irreconcilable; someone must have portrayed Montaigne other than he was. In the absence of any record to the contrary, one can only conclude that Montaigne either never carried out his threat or else is so far behind in his haunting that he may never catch up. And this is reassuring.

The first serious study of Montaigne's thought in its development appeared in 1900. Then Edme Champion in his *Introduction aux "Essais" de Montaigne,* Fortunat Strowski in his *Montaigne* (1906), and above all Pierre Villey in his monumental *Les Sources et l'évolution des "Essais" de Montaigne* (1908) showed with little disagreement and increasing conclusiveness that a chronology of the *Essays* can be established, that many apparent contradictions are really changes of opinion, and that Montaigne's book and his thought can best be understood not as a static monolith but as a growth and an unfolding. Villey's theory may be summed up as follows.

Soon after retiring to his château in 1571, Montaigne began to write. His earliest essays were little more than compilations, such as were popular in his day, of similar or contrasting views or anecdotes, followed by a brief moral. From these, under the influence of Seneca and Plutarch, he turned to writing others in a rather stoical vein, advocating rigid self-mastery and a firm struggle for consistency against the ills of life. His hero was usually Cato the Younger; his concern with preparing to meet pain and death worthily was almost an obsession. This period extends from about 1572 to 1574 and may be called his "stoical period."

A second period or moment in Montaigne's thought is his "skeptical crisis." This may be placed in or around 1576, when he had a medal struck showing a pair of scales in equipoise with his most famous motto underneath: *Que sçay-je?*—"What do I know?" Delighted with the brilliant skepticism of Pyrrho as expounded by Sextus Empiricus, he adopted it for the trenchant critique of human knowledge and reason that constitutes the main part of his longest essay, the "Apology for Raymond Sebond."

The third and final stage in his thought goes from about 1578 to 1592 and is called his "Epicurean period." In it he wrote many essays of Books One and Two and all of Book Three. In these Montaigne realized his immediate purpose of portraying himself and finding the moral laws of his own nature as well as his broader purpose of doing the same for man in general, of whom he found himself not only an interesting but a representative specimen. With ever-growing confidence he preached his doctrine —that we must find our nature and follow it. Convinced that variable man was also pretty inelastic, he urged concentration on simple human goodness rather than on works of stoical or even Christian supererogation; moderation rather than abstention or excess; a balance of duties between oneself and others that is neither selfishness nor unselfishness. The rigidity of Cato gave way as his ideal to the rich versatility, the simple naturalness, the easy goodness of Socrates. Death was no longer an obsession to be fought but a simple eventuality to be dealt with simply when it came. Life was a wonderful opportunity; to live it naturally was the greatest happiness and the highest dignity of man.

This view or a variant of it has been accepted by most Montaigne scholars of the last forty years. A few have opposed it and clung to the notion that the surface inconsistencies in Montaigne are a deliberate veil for dangerous irreligious ideas. But they have left much unexplained; most of their principal arguments have been refuted; and more and more facts recently unearthed have supported the opposite view. A few who in general agree with Villey have criticized him for depending too much on bookish sources or for his use of the terms "stoical" and "Epicurean" but have offered nothing better as a theory.

My own feeling is that the notion of an evolving Montaigne is absolutely indispensable to a good understanding of him, but that its usual form does not bring out adequately the organic quality of the unfolding of his thought. How, for example, does "stoicism" lead to "skepticism," and "skepticism" to "Epicureanism"? How do these relate to the plan of studying himself and man in general? What is the effect on Montaigne's thinking of such cardinal events as the deaths of so many loved relatives and friends, his travels, his experience as mayor and negotiator, and above all his illness? Most of these questions do not seem to have been answered as well as they might be.

Perhaps a more organic theory would show the unfolding of Montaigne's thought as a progressive liberation from apprehension and tutelage. His deep affection for the Christian humanist La Boétie gave him an admiration for stoical humanism that was not quite natural in him and that he had to fight in order to become fully himself. The deaths within ten years of La Boétie, Montaigne's father, an uncle, a brother, and two daughters, and of countless Frenchmen in the religious wars and the Saint Bartholomew's Day massacres, made pain and death, and the duty to prepare to meet them worthily, a near-obsession. But after a few essays in stoical humanism, Montaigne rebelled against it intellectually in the "Apology for Raymond Sebond," where he found it presumptuous, often comical, psychologically unsound, and unfit for himself or any man. The sweeping skepticism of the "Apology" led him to seek the truth not in human reason or in other men but in his judgment and experience of himself; and he made himself the subject of his book. Meanwhile, the fierce pains of the kidney stone attacked him, found him undaunted and still happy, and freed him from apprehension. The success of his first two books of essays, his travels, and his work as mayor of Bordeaux contributed to his awareness of human solidarity and taught him that his individual portrait was also universal. With heightened confidence he set forth the fruits of his judgment and experience, his advice on finding our nature and following it, on living life fully, happily, humanly.

PERMANENCE AND CHANGE

In studying the development of Montaigne's thought we must not, of course, forget the element of permanence. Often he remarks on how little he has changed. "I am nearly always in place, like heavy and inert bodies," he writes. "For the firmest and most general ideas I have are those which, in a manner of speaking, were born with me." In himself as in others he finds a ruling pattern that successfully opposes any radical change. Many views, attitudes, and feelings of the young Montaigne were only confirmed by age and experience. Young or old, he is still Montaigne.

His mental temper, for example, seems always to have been skeptical. Skeptical in the etymological sense of one who judiciously stops to look before he takes a mental leap, who considers all sides before he commits himself. Skeptical because his mind is always more sensitive to diversity than to uniformity; because nature, as he sees it, has made things more unlike than like, so that all comparisons are lame and all statements oversimplifications. Skeptical because his historical and personal perspective always reminds him that the views of his time, his country, and himself are by no means absolute truths. Skeptical from experience and judgment, which have shown him his own intellectual follies and those of others. Skeptical finally because he is deeply aware of the unceasing change in us and in all earthly things which keeps anything constant and permanent like absolute truth from dwelling in us.

But his was not the pure skepticism of unending consideration that never leads to decision or action. His strong poetic streak, the proud impetuosity of the Gascon nobleman, the hard-headed common sense of the son of able merchants—all these kept him from withdrawal into a dubitative shell. Montaigne was a wholly practical man whose dominant concern was living. Thinking is a part of living; but to do nothing but think about living is to be only partly alive. Even if absolute truth is beyond us, there are relative, subjective, human truths that we can live by. Our change and variation is a reason for skepticism; but our experience of it—as Descartes was to see later—is something that we know. Thus experience teaches us to be skeptical and at the same time not to be utterly skeptical. Here as everywhere moderation is the rule.

One realm that Montaigne always places beyond doubt is the Catholic religion. Even the critics who think he undermines it see no change in his attitude. Nor do the majority of his readers, who accept as sincere his theory that skepticism about human knowledge is the securest basis for religious faith. For Montaigne, everything here below is becoming and not being, appearance and not reality. God alone *is:* his truths alone are eternal and absolute. In this rather Platonic dualism there is no way, no ladder of love or progressive abstraction, by which man unaided may climb to the realm of truth. God alone can raise man up, and by his grace, not by any merit of ours. Thus God and his truth, infinitely remote, are as inaccessible and immune to our judgment as to our efforts. It is for God to know and to command, for us to accept and to obey. This fideism of Montaigne, no longer orthodox but acceptable then as a weapon against Protestant exegetical presumption, seems constant. So does his conviction that our helplessness to rise toward God leaves us free to work out our own lives on human terms with a clear conscience.

Again we come back to Montaigne's central concern—man and his life. It is hard to prove just when and how he came to see that he was the subject of his book and that he and man were one, but it is clear that from the first his subject was man, and that he knew it. Few men have been less metaphysical, few less abstract in every way. The here and the now, men and their neighbors, why they behave as they do and how they should behave—these were always his meat, and all else was futile and insipid.

Human conduct is the central point of all. Keen psychologist though he was, Montaigne was always ultimately a moralist. His curiosity was always alert, but his judgment was always waiting to assess and apply the results. All he learned about himself and others was only partly an end in itself. It was also a means to his only final end: to live life well and appropriately, and—when he had learned how—to teach others to do so.

As constant as his central concern is Montaigne's central rule—follow nature. The precise meaning of the phrase may change a little, but the principle remains constant. So do the vices that Montaigne ridicules, notably presumption and her daughter ambition, and those he hates, notably falsity, hypocrisy, treachery, cruelty. Nature is on the other side, that of wisdom, integrity, good humor, and happiness; and so is Montaigne.

But if Montaigne is always Montaigne, still he changes; and he knows it. "I want," he says, "to represent the course of my humors, and for people to see each part at its birth. I wish I had begun earlier, and would take pleasure in recognizing the train of my mutations." Over and over in his late essays he tells how the years have altered him in soul and body and how he is fighting the illusions and excesses of age as he used to fight those of youth. Concerning the first appearance of his *Essays,* in 1580, he writes: "Since then I have grown older by a long stretch of time; but certainly I have not grown an inch wiser. Myself now and myself a while ago are indeed two; but when better, I simply cannot say."

Montaigne knew that he had in him both permanence and change. So long as we do not forget the first, we may now turn to the other.

1

The Young Hedonist
1533-1563

YOUNG MONTAIGNE

WE usually think of Montaigne as a meditative middle-aged man, reading and writing alone in the tower of his manor. This is proper enough, for it was in his last twenty years that he wrote the *Essays* that make him live today. Our knowledge of the first two-thirds of his life is still tantalizingly fragmentary. There are some facts to go on—most of them external—and some judgments and insights, a few by his friend La Boétie, the majority by himself. Most of these need weighing as well as arranging to give a true and clear picture of young Montaigne.

He was born at a bright moment for French humanists and for the peaceful religious reform they sought. Inspired by Erasmus and Lefèvre d'Etaples (Faber Stapulensis), they wanted mainly to know the Bible better through humanistic inquiry and make it available and understandable to all. They were bitterly attacked by the powerful conservative theologians of the Sorbonne but were protected by King Francis I, who had never liked the Sorbonne, and by his sister, Queen Marguerite of Navarre, who was almost a disciple of Lefèvre. To the delight of the evangelistic humanists, Francis had recently founded the first nontheological school of higher learning in France—the school which later became the Collège de France—and he continued to support it against the fury of the conservatives. Rabelais in his *Gargantua* and Marot in his poems could feel secure in mocking the ignorant Sorbonne and hailing the new academy as inaugurating a golden age of learning.

But before Montaigne was two years old the situation changed abruptly. The "Affaire des Placards," the posting of handbills violently attacking the Mass and the papacy, in Paris and even on the king's chamber door at Amboise, on the night of October 17, 1534, was the decisive event; for it convinced Francis that reform had become seditious. Prosecution and persecution began immediately. Calvin fled to prepare his *Institutes* and to build in Geneva a fortress of militant reform. The day of the moderates was past.

It was Calvinism that now spread through France, underground but steadily, until the outbreak of hostilities. Even the violent repressive measures taken by Francis's son Henry II (1547–59) could not halt its growth. His death and that of his son Francis II a year later left the monarchy weak, for his other sons were minors, and his widow Catherine de' Medici, the regent, was a foreigner. The treasury, moreover, was depleted by foreign wars. The Protestants demanded freedom of worship. When Catherine and her chancellor, Michel de l'Hospital, granted it to them, Catholic opinion was outraged. A colloquy was held at Poissy (October, 1561) to try to reconcile the doctrinal differences, but it only emphasized them. Incidents on both sides, such as the attempt to capture the Catholic leader François de Guise, fanned the flames of violence that were already raging. When Guise was provoked by some of his Protestant subjects who were worshiping illegally at Vassy (March 1, 1562), he and his men attacked them, wounded over a hundred, and killed over twenty. Alarmed Protestant leaders raised troops, and open war began.

Though Montaigne grew up in this atmosphere of mounting tension, he seems to have remained for his first thirty years an observer, concerned but not involved. He was born on February 28, 1533, of a line of important Bordeaux merchants ennobled since

1477 by the purchase of the "noble land" of Montaigne on a breezy hill in the Dordogne valley region between Bordeaux and Périgueux. His father, Pierre Eyquem de Montaigne, he dearly loved; of his mother, *née* Antoinette de Louppes, he almost never speaks. She too was of prosperous merchant stock; her family were converted Spanish Jews well established in Bordeaux. Two or three of their eight children became Protestants; Michel and the rest remained Catholics like their parents.

When Michel Eyquem de Montaigne—he was later to drop the bourgeois name Eyquem—was born, two older brothers had already died. His father, a vigorous, original man who had served in the wars in Italy and was alive to new ideas, gave his full attention to bringing up his oldest surviving son. To draw him close to humble folk, Michel had peasant godparents and was sent out to nurse at a nearby village. On his return nothing was spared to make his life pleasant; hardly ever punished, he was even awakened every morning by music. To teach him Latin easily and well—he and his father later picked up a little Greek as a game—he was put in the charge of a German tutor who knew no French, and of two assistants, and heard nothing but Latin spoken until he was six. At the Collège de Guyenne in Bordeaux, where he spent the next seven years, even the best Latinists of a brilliant faculty feared to accost him, so fluent was he; and he played leading roles with great enjoyment in some of their Latin plays. However, despite his father's special arrangements, he found here the seamy side of education—monotony, pointless confinement, severity and even cruelty in punishment: "a real jail of captive youth." His Latin grew rusty; all he got out of this schooling was a fondness for a few authors such as Ovid, Virgil, Terence, and Plautus, whom a wise private tutor put in his way and lured him into reading on the sly.

Of the next eight years of Montaigne's life (1546–54) we know only that he must have studied law—probably at Toulouse—and that at the age of fifteen he witnessed in Bordeaux an act of mob violence that he was never to forget. The governor, M. de Moneins, tried to go from one safe place to another through streets full of townspeople ready for riot. His action, Montaigne tells us, may not have been unwise; but his woeful lack of assurance incited the mob, and he was killed. Years later, as mayor of Bordeaux, Montaigne was to remember this lesson and meet a similar situation successfully with a firm and confident demeanor.

In 1554 the king created a new court in Périgueux, the Cour des Aides, to deal with special tax cases, and also to bring in money to the treasury from the customary sale of the newly-created offices. Montaigne's father bought himself a place and promptly resigned it in favor of his son to take up his new duties as mayor of Bordeaux. The new court was opposed so strongly that three years later the king dissolved it and ordered its members to be accepted into the Parlement of Bordeaux. Though they were most grudgingly received, young Montaigne thus became at twenty-four a member of a very important body, in which he remained for thirteen years. Less powerful than the Paris Parlement because less central, the regional parlements had the same rights and functions. New edicts needed their promulgation to be carried out in their districts; in times of trouble they had much to do in support—theoretically at least—of the royal authority. Primarily, however, they were the king's judicial arm. The Bordeaux Parlement, comprising many learned and distinguished men, was divided into two main chambers and a third smaller one. Though their actions were taken jointly, the Chambre des Enquêtes mainly prepared and reported on cases, whereas the Grand'Chambre handed down the decisions. Montaigne began, as was natural, in the Chambre des Enquêtes, and to his chagrin was never able to change.

His years as a magistrate seem to have been a mixed experience but mainly a bad one. Although this was a fairly good court, still there was some corruption and hypocrisy, much cruelty and inequity, and too much pomp and ceremony. Once in the *Essays,* starting to write a little about himself, Montaigne says he finds himself "entangled in the laws of ceremony" and decides to "let her alone for the moment." That was possible in his book, but easier said than done in the Parlement of Bordeaux.

Certainly he was absent much of the time—by permission, to be sure—at the court of the king, mostly on missions but on missions that he had requested. It is positively known that he made nine such trips before his retirement; it is likely that he went about once a year. Here was a gayer and more exciting life than in the Parlement, with history being made before your eyes; this had a great appeal to the young Gascon gentleman. But here, too, you could not be yourself; there you were a machine, here a mask.

Only one unmixed blessing came to Montaigne from these long years: his friendship with Etienne de La Boétie. Even this did not last, for after four or five years his friend died young. With his death ended a period in Montaigne's life.

In trying to picture young Montaigne we must avoid two opposite extremes. The sage of fifty was not a sage in his twenties. Nor was he on the other hand as gay, heedless, and lascivious as we might assume from certain remarks in La Boétie's verses and later in the *Essays.* All these remarks must be judged in context. The verses are monitory, not descriptive; no giddy reprobate could have been the bosom friend of the high-minded La Boétie. When Montaigne tells us of his wanton youth, he is aging, failing in body, struggling to avoid going sour; almost all his descriptions are in terms of contrast, and exaggerated. When he defends the wisdom of youth against that of age, however, he gives us a more balanced picture that seems more reliable.

Montaigne as a boy stands well revealed in the essay "Of the Education of Children" (I:26). Independent and tenacious but slow to move, he was in danger of doing not wrong, but nothing at all—a reproach he was to hear all his life. Secure in the intelligent love of the father he loved dearly in return, he spent a boyhood generally happy but marred by his first seven years of formal education. These gave him his first real taste of folly and injustice; and from what he tells us of his mind at the time, he may well even then have judged much as he did later the inanity and severity that could come of knowledge and authority misapplied. No matter what his father did, "it was still school."

Montaigne's Catholicism must have been the result of a real decision. When this came, we do not know, nor even just when his brother and sister—or possibly two sisters—were converted to Protestantism. But his father was presumably concerned about the matter by the time Montaigne was thirteen, for it was no later than that that his friend Bunel gave him Sebond's "Book of Creatures, or Natural Theology" as a support for Catholics against heresy. Many young nobles in the fifteen-forties and fifties, for love of adventure and many other reasons, had at least a mild flirtation with the new cult. Montaigne himself was somewhat drawn to it in its days of adversity and at one time tended to scout certain points of Catholic doctrine. His independence of mind makes one wonder what were his exact reasons for remaining in the fold. The Protestants had not yet done the harm that he was to emphasize later. Earlier it may have been intellectual conviction, premonition of trouble to come, skepticism about new ideas, allegiance to the faith of his father, or some combination of these and perhaps still other motives. We can only conjecture which ones were dominant. But in a family so divided, Montaigne's decision was an important one.

From thirteen to twenty-one, from schoolboy to fledgling magistrate, Montaigne is almost lost from sight. We have a better picture, fragmentary but suggestive, of his sixteen years in the courts of Périgueux and Bordeaux. We know how shabbily the newcomers were received in Bordeaux; that their due precedence was long denied and often challenged, even when at last acknowledged; and that on one such occasion Montaigne spoke out for the first time, tersely, to point out that their precedence had already been recognized in fact. We sense from the *Essays* how much he learned in the Parlement: the broad experience of human behavior, especially of sham and cussedness, the "capacity to sift the truth," weighing evidence and probing into motivation, the conviction that however undemonstrable the standard, things were either right or wrong, and that thoughtful investigation and understanding must lead ultimately to right judgment.

More conspicuous than the profit was the vexation. It was bad enough to be confined mainly to reporting and not judging; it was worse that even this had to be based not on equity but on the interpretation of a cumbersome and often unfair body of law. The *Essays* are full of Montaigne's direct comments:

> Consider the form of this justice that governs us: it is a true testimony of human imbecility, so full it is of contradiction and error. . . . Poor devils are sacrificed to the forms of justice. . . . How many condemnations I have seen which were more criminal than the crime. . . .
>
> Now laws remain in credit not because they are just, but because they are laws. . . . They are often made by fools, more often by people who, in their hatred of equality, are wanting in equity; but always by men, vain and irresolute authors.
>
> There is nothing so grossly and widely and ordinarily defective as the laws. Whoever obeys them because they are just does not obey them for just the right reason.

Here is at least one source of Montaigne's constant vexation with ceremony, of his awareness of human injustice, and most important, of his skepticism. It did not take Sextus Empiricus to teach him the vanity of the human intellect; he had learned it for sixteen hard years.

The outstanding characteristic of the young Montaigne as seen by his older self is independence. Brought up to freedom and adaptability, he "loves to give his freedom elbow room in all directions." He hates to feel indebted, or even to ask favors, because of "a little natural pride, inability to take refusal, contraction of my desires and designs, inability in all sorts of affairs, and my most favorite qualities—idleness, freedom." Almost equally he hates to involve himself unnecessarily or excessively. Few things grip him, and he has cultivated this inborn trait: temperamentally incapable of solicitude, he would lend his blood as readily as his care. By nature and by reason he is frank. He would rather be importunate and indiscreet than a dissimulating flatterer. Even in his amours he is wholly honest, indeed blunt, in his approaches. Impatient of any constraint, he learns better from contrast than example, from good fortune than bad. Even the constraint of habit he has trained himself to avoid. Never that he can remember has he taken advice —nor often given it. He sees the illusions of age as well as those of youth. Impatient as a youngster when people competing with him would not try their hardest, he has always wanted to be treated as a man and felt that he should be. Too much is made of mere seniority, he thinks. We should be used earlier in public office. If we have any stuff in us to show, we have shown it at twenty.

Not all his traits of temperament are easy to assort. As is natural, he seems somewhat less phlegmatic early than late. He takes little trouble, he tells us, to correct his natural inclinations. Rather gay than melancholy, his native good spirits are tinged with seriousness but not sadness. He is lively; his legs are full of quicksilver; it is a good sermon that can keep him still and attentive. He is impetuous: even in his later years he eats greedily and sometimes bites his fingers in the process; once, when challenged in the Parlement, he replies with what the official report describes as "all the vivacity of his character." Though not an ambitious man, he is by no means free from ambition, as indeed he is never to be. Even his study as a youth, he says, is for ostentation, as are certain purchases of books. He is neither truly gregarious nor a pure solitary: his nature is outgoing and communicative. Altogether, his best quality of temperament is a full firm vigor.

Not a big man but solid, lively and full of health, a touch of pride showing in certain gestures, he is careless with his money, gay and debonair, imaginative, a lover of poetry, of adornment, of excitement and variety. In short, a typical well-adjusted young man setting out to conquer the world and enjoy it. The splendor of the court draws him again and again in his twenties. Judging by the volume of his confidences on his youth, he is drawn most of all to the pursuit of women.

His attitude toward them is not completely simple. Like so many of the ancients and of his own contemporaries, he generally regards them as potentially decorative lightweights, incapable either of good sense or of mental or spiritual elevation. True friendship is beyond their reach; their love is nothing but sexual gratification. Constitutionally enslaved either to passion or to prudery, they have been denied by nature the freedom that allows some men to attain the dignity of fully human living. The essay "Of Three Good Women" (II:35), which is pointedly followed by "Of the Most Excellent Men," begins "They don't come by the dozen, as everyone knows"; and the goodness of the three heroines consists simply in great devotion to their husbands.

Yet Montaigne likes them and wants to be liked by them. The several essays that he dedicates he dedicates to women; their society is one of the three associations that he enjoys. And his most licentious essay, "On Some Verses of Virgil," written, he says, so that women will take his book from their salons into their boudoirs, concludes that men have been unfair to them and kept them from their rightful equality. His usual attitude in the *Essays,* which is mainly that of his fifties, is the affectionate condescension of maturity toward the charm and folly of adolescence.

In his youth his dominant feeling apparently is frank desire.

He says he cannot remember when he was a virgin; he can imagine chastity but has never practiced it. He has suffered the flame and pangs of love. Though he has avoided paid amours, he has not escaped a bout or two of venereal disease. No professional ladies' man, always perfectly frank in his affairs, he will not stoop to deceit. Sexual intercourse he greatly enjoys as a healthy, natural, and therefore legitimate function. If he seems to treat it rather like eating, at least he finds it much more exciting.

Altogether, it is a lively young magistrate that the *Essays* fondly evoke. Yet his liveliness is not giddy. Even as later he fights the illusions of age, so now he fights those of youth. While his passions disport, his judgment remains an uncommitted observer. Looking back later on his youthful amours, he finds that he had himself pretty well in hand and would do no better now if exposed to such strong temptation. He is prudent in concealment when necessary. By an effort he can oppose his passions with diversion and reason; he can recognize the face of vice under the mask of pleasure. Independent above all, he vigorously and successfully fights any bondage to love: "In this business, I did not wholly let myself go; I enjoyed it, but I did not forget myself; I kept in its entirety that bit of sense and discretion that nature gave me, to the advantage of my partners and to mine: a bit of emotion, but no folly."

Besides judgment and self-control, another serious trait marks the young Montaigne. Whatever he did, he says, death was never far from his thoughts. We can only guess at the cause of this near-obsession. Certainly it is not uncommon in youth, to whose long, long thoughts the limits as well as the possibilities of life often seem closer and more real than they do later. Montaigne does not let death worry him, but he feels its nearness constantly:

> There is nothing with which I have at all ages more occupied my mind than with images of death. Even in the most licentious season of my age . . . amid ladies and games, someone would think me involved

in digesting some jealousy by myself, or the uncertainty of some hope, while I was thinking about I don't remember whom, who had been overtaken a few days before by a hot fever and by death, on leaving a similar feast, his head full of idleness, love, and a happy time, like myself; and that the same chance was hanging from my ear. . . . I did not wrinkle my forehead any more over that thought than any other. . . . Otherwise for my part I would have been in continual fear and frenzy; for never did a man so distrust his life, never did a man set less faith in his duration.

LA BOÉTIE

Into the life of this gay but reflective young hedonist there came a friend, Etienne de La Boétie. Montaigne was twenty-five or twenty-six, La Boétie two and a third years older. His father was a prominent official in the town of Sarlat, his mother the sister of a president of the Parlement of Bordeaux. To this court he was admitted at twenty-two, three years before the legal age, after excellent law studies at Orléans. Soon distinguished by his intelligence, integrity, and assiduity, he was charged with missions of considerable importance. He was married and settled, nobly ambitious, sure of his standards and aims in life. A passionate humanist and admirer of the Pléiade poets, he had written verse himself in Latin as well as French and won praise for it from such critics as Baïf and Scaliger. What concerned him most, however, was the public welfare; what he admired most in ancient Rome was the morale and organization of the Republic. His chief claim to literary fame was an eloquent treatise against tyranny, written probably in his teens and later revised, entitled "Discourse on Voluntary Servitude" and often referred to as the *Contr'un.* Almost equally great was his concern with philosophy, especially moral philosophy, where his position was that of most humanists of his time, a blend of stoicism and Christianity.

Such is the friend whom Montaigne describes as the greatest all-round man he has known. Before we smile too broadly at this bit of friendly bias, we may do well to remember that if Montaigne had died when La Boétie did and been survived and praised in these terms by his friend, we would have been more incredulous still.

Their relationship, which both men place beyond compare, is described by Montaigne in an essay unique for warmth and eloquence, "Of Friendship" (I:28). They had heard of each other before they met: "we embraced each other," says Montaigne, "by our names." From their very first meeting at a large public occasion they were bound together for life. Starting so comparatively late, they had no time to lose in ceremony. They knew and trusted each other utterly; all that each had was for the other. The considerations that brought them together are beyond analysis for Montaigne: it was some quintessence of them all that led each to lose his will in the other's. "If you press me to tell why I loved him, I feel that this cannot be expressed, except by answering: Because it was he, because it was I."

When La Boétie died in 1563, Montaigne was inconsolable. "I only drag on a weary life," he writes. "And the very pleasures that come my way, instead of consoling me, redouble my grief for his loss. We went halves in everything; it seems to me that I am robbing him of his share. . . . I was already so formed and accustomed to being a second self everywhere that only half of me seems to be alive now. . . . There is no action or thought in which I do not miss him, as indeed he would have missed me. For just as he surpassed me infinitely in every other ability and virtue, so he did in the duty of friendship."

That La Boétie felt the same way is clear from the second of two Latin poems which he addressed to Montaigne. Their main interest to us here, however, is in the picture they offer of Montaigne in his late twenties. The subject of the first (72 lines) is an ancient fable: the meeting of Hercules with Virtue and Pleasure, at which Virtue showed him the ugliness of her rival and the glorious difficulty of following herself. The second is a detailed account (322 lines) of the miseries of adultery, in which Montaigne defends his eagerness for this sport and La Boétie replies. Though Montaigne appears more attracted to vice than immersed in it, it is obvious that idleness and voluptuousness are his greatest dangers.

But through the exaggerated praise traditional in such poems, Montaigne's promise shows equally clearly. His friend compares him to a Cyclops, an Alcibiades, twice to a Hercules, and calls him eager and alert, able and free, "with winged foot already near the goal, about to pluck the crowns." He describes himself as ordinary, inferior to Montaigne in friendship and mediocre in virtue. But his friend will soon vie with the highest, for his possibilities are infinite. Like Alcibiades, however, Montaigne appears equally apt for virtue and vice. Ladies smile at him; the world is his oyster. He is noble and rich, vigorous and free, so happy, proud, and passionate that it is hard for a young friend to advise him. "Shall I bend," Montaigne protests, "with sleepless care, to harass all these volumes? Shall I alone, now that I am older, be ignorant of Venus? My house supplies ample riches, my age ample powers. Surely here is the proper use of wealth and verdant youth." All La Boétie can do is fight a delaying action by showing the pains and ugliness of adultery and the pure beauty of virtuous labor.

As seen in his late twenties through his friend's eyes, Montaigne appears more like himself at fifty-five than at forty. Much as he loves virtue, he wants no curtailment of life or freedom. He mistrusts conventional and ready-made standards—the intrinsic value of labor and of learning, any categorical bans on pleasure. Quite obviously he has thought about these things; he is ready to defend his ideas, and his friend must pick his arguments carefully. Though La Boétie's estimate is probably generous, Montaigne's mind must already be extremely sure and keen to elicit such praise, especially since as far as we know his ability is still unpublished. Independence and solidity alone do not explain his friend's assurance of his promise. Already he seems to be what he will be ten years later—a man of great ability in search of his function.

The differences between the two men are clear and sizable. La Boétie stands for a more rigid moral code, more labor, more thirst for glory; Montaigne admires these things but also questions them. However, they have a great deal in common besides the friendship itself. They probably shared a number of ideas that La Boétie alone expresses this early but that Montaigne later develops with no hint of change or variation. Among these are the views on religion and the state which La Boétie sets forth in his "Memoir Concerning the Edict of January 1562."

This edict was the first attempt by Catherine de' Medici and L'Hospital to conciliate the Protestants by giving them considerable rights. War had probably broken out when La Boétie wrote to criticize this tolerance, not for theological but for civil reasons. Two religions, he says, can only breed strife and impair the king's authority. Every concession by the crown has weakened it and increased the arrogant demands of the common people, who are no fit judges in these matters. Huguenots in France and Protestants in Germany are proof that toleration does not pay. Yet the government continues to pile concession upon concession.

The alternative is a single creed, and that can only be the Catholic: the king could not in conscience have it otherwise. First certain Protestant leaders should be severely punished for their rebellion. Then the worst abuses within the Catholic Church should be reformed. Superficial differences between the sects should be reconciled. Finally, Protestantism should be abolished in France. All this should be done by the king, acting mainly through his parlements.

Two actions strongly suggest that Montaigne already, as in the *Essays* later, sympathized strongly with these intolerant but clear-sighted opinions of what the welfare of France demanded. One concerned a recently revived oath of fidelity to Catholicism that he had to take in order to sit with the Paris Parlement on June 12, 1562. It is not surprising that he took it, but it is noteworthy that he did so with an eagerness that pleased the court. Late in the next year, soon after La Boétie's death, the First President of the Bordeaux Parlement, Lagebaston, a protégé and supporter of L'Hospital, was protested as a judge on a certain case by the anti-tolerationist seneschal of Guyenne, Escars. La Boétie had been a friend of Escars, at whose home he had contracted his fatal illness. When Lagebaston in turn protested several of his colleagues, including Montaigne, as working for Escars, Montaigne did not deny the charge but replied "with all the vivacity of his character."

As for the main general humanistic ideas about life and death, Montaigne seems to have clung to his independence against his living friend but surrendered it for a while at the beauty of his death. We have a glimpse of their discussions in an early essay, when Montaigne writes that he has always held, "against the opinion of many, and even of Etienne de La Boétie," that dying people did not really suffer very badly if they were in a coma. Our main view is in Montaigne's moving account of his friend's last days, which he wrote, apparently soon after, in a letter to his father, and published in 1570 at the end of the volume of La Boétie's works.

On August 9, 1563, La Boétie came down with some sort of intestinal grippe from overexposure after exercise, just as he was about to make a trip to Médoc. Many of his neighbors in Bordeaux had come down with the plague. After consulting with Montaigne, he went a bit of the way to stay with friends at Germignan, which was safer than his home. Early the next morning his wife sent for Montaigne, saying that her husband was badly ill. For five days, while Montaigne was with him off and on, he grew steadily worse. Then he told his friend to beware of the gloominess and possible contagion of his disease. "He asked me," says Montaigne, "to be with him only for short visits, but as often as I could. I did not leave him again."

On the Sunday, the seventh day, La Boétie had a spell of great weakness, with cloudy and chaotic visions, not painful, but in his judgment surely no better than death. Beginning to lose hope of getting well, he accepted Montaigne's suggestion that he put his affairs in order, and urged him in case of death to control by his wisdom his own grief and that of La Boétie's beloved wife and uncle. He told these three in general of his will, which left his books to Montaigne, and of his gratitude for all their help and love. Now he was free to consider his conscience. "I am a Christian," he said, "I am a Catholic; so have I lived, so do I intend to end my life. Send for a priest, for I do not want to fail in this last duty of a Christian."

At this point he looked so much better that Montaigne had a flash of hope. But it did not last; shortly they settled down to the slow bleak task of preparing for La Boétie's death. Here is Montaigne's report of some of their talk:

> But two or three hours later, both to keep up in him this greatness of courage, and also because I wished, in the jealousy I have had all my life for his glory and honor, that there should be more witnesses of so many fine proofs of greatness of soul, by there being more people in his room: I told him that I had blushed for shame that my courage had failed on hearing what he, who was involved in this illness, had had the courage to tell me. That up to then I had thought that God gave no such great advantage over human accidents, and I had difficulty believing what I sometimes read about it in the histories; but that having felt such a proof of it, I praised God that this had been in a person by whom I was so loved and whom I loved so dearly; and that this would serve me as an example, to play this same part in my turn.
>
> He interrupted me to beg me to use it in this way, and to show in action that the talks we had had together during our health had been borne not merely in our mouths but deeply engraved on heart and in

soul, so as to put them into execution at the first occasions that should be offered; adding that this was the true practice of our studies, and of philosophy.

This trial of his, La Boétie went on, was not so hard: "I had been prepared for it for a long time, and known my lesson all by heart." Already he had lived long enough, healthy and happy, simply and without malice. Life being uncertain, his could hardly have lasted much longer, and much that he was now to miss would not have been good. Now he was going to see God and the abode of the blest.

Here Montaigne faltered, and La Boétie had to encourage him. The notary came, and the will was drawn up. La Boétie bade farewell to his niece and stepdaughter, commending them to virtue, and then in private to Montaigne's brother Beauregard. Apologizing first for speaking freely, he said he knew that Beauregard was a sincere and zealous Protestant spurred to revolt by the vices of the Catholic Church. But for the sake of his house and the will of his good father, his uncle, and his brothers, he should shun these extremes: "Do not be so bitter and so violent; be reconciled with them. Do not make band and body apart; be joined together. You see how much ruin these dissensions have brought to this kingdom, and I warrant you they will bring still greater."

On the next day La Boétie was much worse, and even reproached Montaigne for adding to his pain by bringing him back to consciousness and keeping him alive. He took confession, and on the following day heard Mass; prayed God to help him and end his pain soon; and asked his uncle and Montaigne to pray for him, too. Two or three times he suddenly called out: "All right! all right! Let it come when it wants, I'm waiting for it, strong and firm of foot." He tried to tell his friend of the visions he saw but could say only, "Great, great," and later: "they are marvelous, infinite, and ineffable." When his wife's tears grew too strong, he comforted her and sent her away, saying that he was going off—

going off, he added quickly, to sleep. Delirious, he asked Montaigne over and over to make a place for him, and was told in reply that he had one already. "True, true," he said, "but it is not the one I need." Early on Wednesday morning, August 18, 1563, he died quietly in his bed, having lived, as Montaigne concludes, thirty-two years, nine months, and seventeen days.

It is a commonplace in eulogies of Montaigne that his friend still lives in the *Essays*. It is also profoundly true. The influence of La Boétie on Montaigne, in life and in death, is simply enormous. The moving chapter on friendship, set in the center of Book One and worked over with loving care as a setting for La Boétie's "Voluntary Servitude," is no mere exercise in rhetoric. When Montaigne says that with his friend dead he feels only half alive, he means it.

Much of his later life is colored by his friendship and his loss. For two years he sought to divert his grief in various amours. Then, partly perhaps as a corrective for these, he married; and since for him a good marriage (if such there be) was modeled on friendship, his probably suffered by comparison. When he resigned from the Parlement, where his friend no longer sat, his first task was to publish La Boétie's remaining works, severally, with careful dedications to important persons. In these and in the early essays he seems to consider himself as primarily the guardian of his friend's memory. But for him, he tells us, La Boétie's meaning would have been torn in a thousand contrary directions. Whatever his own promise for the future, he seems to believe that his greatest achievement up to then has been to share such a bond with such a man.

In retirement he sought not so much solitude itself as detachment from the overdependence on others that makes us suffer so when we lose them. His decision to write arose, he says, from a melancholy humor unusual in him, caused by the gloom of his solitude; this can hardly have been unrelated to his bereavement.

And the *Essays,* with their frank, first-person, conversational style, are in a very real sense a substitute for his friendship, an outlet for his need of communication, a bottle—or many bottles —in the sea. If a copy should reach a man who would like to be a real friend, he writes wistfully in his fifties, he would gladly travel anywhere to offer him essays in flesh and blood.

Eighteen years after La Boétie's death, Montaigne fell to thinking of him once as he was writing a letter in Rome. The thought made him so sad that it caused him real pain. To the sage, he tells us later in the *Essays,* a dead friend is as present twenty-five years after as when he was alive. So it was with Montaigne.

The influence of La Boétie is unquestionable in the stoical humanism of the early essays; his dying words sound again in "To Philosophize Is to Learn to Die." In so far as this influence grew dominant at any one moment, that seems to be the moment of his death. Only then did Montaigne realize how bravely and nobly a man could die. Only then, apparently, did he fully resolve to accept the long preparation needed to learn his lesson by heart, too, and to play the same part in his turn.

Many other serious losses by death were soon to follow, but this, as far as we know, was the first. The blow, the shock of death in one so young, the noble example, and his own resolve, mark a turning point for Montaigne from carefree hedonism to apprehensive humanism.

◆§ 2 §◆

The Apprehensive Humanist
1563-1573

DEATH ON ALL SIDES

THE religious wars, which had broken out a year and a half before La Boétie's death, were to involve Montaigne deeply and to form the somber background of the last half of his life. There were intervals of comparative peace, some of them rather long. But they were never better than armed truces, for no settlement could satisfy both sides, and during most of them sporadic violence continued in one part of France or another. The Protestants were never comparable in numbers to the Catholics; but these were sharply divided, with the government generally holding to a policy at first of tolerance, then of moderation, while the extremists opposed all concessions. After three wars lasting each a year or two, the Reformists reached their highest peak of influence when their leader Coligny came to court in 1570 and gained great favor with King Charles IX. But the Catholics grew alarmed as Coligny pressed for armed intervention in the Protestant Netherlands against Catholic Spain. When thousands of Protestants flocked into Paris for the marriage of Henry of Navarre, tension rose. When a hired assassin wounded Coligny, it became explosive. Threats flew back and forth, and the king was finally persuaded by his mother, his brother, and others to order the terrible Massacre of St. Bartholomew's Day (August 24, 1572), in which Coligny and thousands of other Protestants were killed.

Navarre was forced to abjure his Protestantism and remain at court, almost a prisoner, until his party regained its strength.

In these first ten years of war, and later too, southwest France was a center of trouble. Béarn and parts of Gascony and Guyenne were deeply Protestant, and nearly everywhere opinion was divided. In the region around the court of Navarre at Nérac there were always Protestant soldiers, and often armies. Catholic Bordeaux, sixty or seventy miles to the northwest, was in a state of almost constant alarm. Most members of the Parlement favored a sterner policy than the government usually did; those who did not were often in hot water with their colleagues. In one period of a year and a half (March, 1569–August, 1570), the court condemned over 1,200 people to death—*in absentia,* to be sure. Again and again it assigned its members to actual police duties for the preservation of law and order.

Montaigne had taken from the first the position of determined loyalism that he never changed. We have noted already his anger at the more compromising Lagebaston soon after La Boétie's death, and his willing oath of fidelity in Paris the year before. In October of that same year (1562) he was with the king's army at the siege of Protestant Rouen; it was there that he met his Brazilian cannibals. And in December, 1567, he wrote from his château a letter to his friend Belot to be read in Parlement, warning them of the passage of Protestant troops. All his actions suggest that, like La Boétie, he regarded the Reformists as primarily rebels against their country and their king.

Meanwhile, after a diversionary sowing of wild oats, Montaigne married, settled down, inherited his father's estate, translated a long theological treatise, requested and was refused more meaningful employment in the Parlement, resigned his position there, published La Boétie's works, retired to his manor, and started to write his *Essays.*

He married Françoise de la Chassaigne, daughter of a conservative president of the Parlement (September 25, 1565), on his father's urging and without enthusiasm, as a social obligation. He would have avoided marrying Wisdom herself, he says, if she had wanted him. Domestic economy was not his dish, nor building, which his father had enjoyed. What he wanted of his home was freedom and peace, and apparently he did not always get them. For all their children, the marriage lacked intimacy and warmth, and Montaigne's remarks about it are generally caustic. It has even been argued plausibly that his wife was unfaithful to him, and with his brother at that. With the possible exception of the early years, the marriage seems to have gone best when each partner had the most privacy.

Montaigne's translation is interesting in many ways. In 1546 or earlier his father had had a visit from Pierre Bunel, one of his admired humanists, who left with him, as an antidote for the Lutheranism that he saw spreading in France, the Latin "Book of Creatures, or Natural Theology" of the fifteenth-century Spaniard Raymond Sebond. Some time before the death of Adrianus Turnebus in 1565 Montaigne himself had shown an interest in the book by asking him about it. Though Pierre de Montaigne knew Latin, and though there was already a French translation and also an adaptation, he asked his son to translate it, which he did. The book appeared in 1569; the dedication to Montaigne's father is dated from Paris, June 18, 1568—the day his father died.

The thousand pages of the "Natural Theology" are an elaborate demonstration of the existence and nature of God by the analogies observable in his creation. From man's superiority to the lower levels of creatures—animal, vegetable, inanimate—God's superiority is elucidated. The book opens with a preface, or prologue, claiming that it is virtually infallible and more useful than the Scriptures. In 1558 or 1559 the book was put on the Index of Prohibited Books; the body of the work was removed from the Index in 1564, but the Prologue was retained.

Montaigne showed great skill in his first literary labor. The translation is smoother and gayer than the original. As he says, he has decked it out a bit, *à la françoise*. But he has fully understood his author and rendered his meaning faithfully—at least throughout the now innocent body of the book.

Not so in the peccant Prologue. Montaigne cuts all Sebond's extravagant claims down to size. "Necessary" becomes "useful"; "infallibly" disappears. The book no longer claims to teach "all the truth necessary to man" (about God and man) but "the truth, so far as this is possible for natural reason"; not the knowledge "necessary to man" but the knowledge "necessary to man before all others." This superb Latinist and faithful translator has deliberately mistranslated in at least twenty places, always to attenuate the presumption of the author's claims.

Many explanations of this fact are possible. Almost certainly Montaigne knew that the Prologue was on the Index. Clearly he wanted his translation to be wholly orthodox—as indeed it was; it was never troubled by censure. There may even be some influence of his father. At all events, Montaigne clearly appears at this time to have been a thinking and conforming Catholic, willing to undertake a sizable literary chore if his father thought it might help the good cause or work for conciliation between the warring sects. And already he was highly skeptical of the power of unaided human reason in matters divine. The germ of the "Apology for Raymond Sebond" exists already in Montaigne's version of the Prologue to the "Natural Theology."

His father's death made Montaigne head of the family and lord of his domain. A little over a year later, with his first child on the way, he sought to rise in the Parlement of Bordeaux from the Chambre des Enquêtes to the Grand'Chambre. Since he had relatives in each of the higher two chambers—a brother-in-law and a father-in-law—his request was denied; and he did not appeal to the king for the necessary dispensation. A year later he sold his position in the court to Florimond de Roemond. He then went to Paris to see to the publication of La Boétie's works, and returned to his château to make his official retirement. He seems to have appeared twice in Paris soon after in connection with the publication. In his early retirement he received two honors from Charles IX—the order of Saint Michel, which he had long coveted, from the hands of Gaston de Foix, marquis de Trans (October 18, 1571), and that of gentleman in ordinary of the king's chamber (some time before October 5, 1573).

These were ten hard years for him. Besides the public bloodshed and alarm, which was terrible in Guyenne, he had private grounds for grief and apprehension. In 1561, without warning, his father had fallen grievously ill with the kidney stone, which after seven painful years was to kill him. Montaigne's own fear of the stone, which grew intense until experience cured it, probably goes back to the early days of his father's suffering. Two years later his beloved friend had been mortally stricken in his thirty-third year. Five years afterward, while Montaigne was away, his father died in great pain. Now that Montaigne for the first time had money of his own, even this began to worry him. Soon after his father, a brother, Arnaud de Saint-Martin, a brave young captain of twenty-three, died as a result of being hit over the ear by a tennis ball. In the same period Montaigne came close to death in the most unlikely way—an accidental collision on horseback; this, too, was a reminder. Another two years, and Thoinette was born, his long-awaited first child, to live only two months. A second child, born in the next year (1571), survived; but in 1573 a third child died an infant, and later still another and another and another. "When these examples, so frequent and so ordinary, pass before our eyes," Montaigne writes of his brother's death, "how is it possible that one can get rid of the thought of death, and that at every instant it should not seem to us that she holds us by the throat?"

THE HUMANIST RETIRES

As Montaigne made his formal entry into retirement on his thirty-eighth birthday, death seemed all around him, and he was doubtful that much was left in life. He had served respectably in the Parlement but failed of the chance for important work there. He had made himself available at court, but—it would appear—no one had used him much. He had done a competent translation, but nothing of his own. The promise that his friend had seen in him was unfulfilled and showed no signs of fulfillment. If indeed he had more brilliance than his friend, he had accomplished less.

Now he was on the shelf; ahead lay old age and death. All he really had to show for his youth was his friendship; and that again led his mind back to death. Death, La Boétie had said, is the test of our studies, our philosophies, our very lives; and what he had said he had lived out. He had made his own passing a heroic example. Montaigne's death would be a test of his friendship, and he must not let down his friend, their friendship, his own best self. He might not accomplish much else: he was past the middle of the journey, and the end seemed very near. Now he must use his leisure to compose and strengthen himself, to prepare to meet death in a way worthy of La Boétie. To fail in this would be the ultimate failure, leaving his life mere nonsense and even his friendship tainted. In this he must not fail.

Such solemn thoughts were probably in his mind as he commemorated his retirement by having painted, on his library wall, the following inscription: "In the year of Christ 1571, at the age of thirty-eight, on the last day of February, anniversary of his birth, Michel de Montaigne, long weary of the servitude of the court and of public employments, while still entire, retired to the bosom of the learned virgins, where in calm and freedom from all cares he will spend what little remains of his life now more than half run out. If the fates permit he will complete this abode, this sweet ancestral retreat; and he has consecrated it to his freedom, tranquillity, and leisure."

The striking thing about this inscription is its humanism. Written, of course, in Latin, rather solemn and pretentious, suitably equipped with fates and muses, it expresses a familiar classical theme well assimilated by an apt pupil. Horace and his countrymen had taught Montaigne how one should feel about retirement and how to express it. He knew that books are the best friends of the intelligent man and that consolation for a somewhat disappointing life is to be found in the bosom of the learned muses.

Montaigne at this point seems to have been less a stoical thinker, whom a skeptical crisis was soon to make more Epicurean, than a humanist who was soon to become skeptical of traditional humanism as a basis for life and to turn from it to the human values that he found within himself. He was a humanist in one of the few clear and accepted senses of the term—a lover of Greek and Roman antiquity and of humane letters, eager to learn the wisdom of the ancient masters.

To be sure, sixteenth-century French humanism was permeated with stoicism, as indeed was all French thought of the time. With religious corruption and Reform contributing to divorce ethics from metaphysics in men's minds and make man more than ever the center of the universe, with heroism and bloodshed the order of the day, the virility, rigor, and tension of stoicism had great appeal. The *Enchiridion* of Epictetus was widely read, as was Marcus Aurelius in Guevara's edition of his *Golden Book*. The heroic figures of Plutarch's *Lives,* translated by Amyot, captured the imagination of all. Cicero and Seneca were tremendously popular and influential. Among those who edited, translated, or commented on Cicero were Etienne Dolet, Julius Caesar Scaliger, Antonio de Gouvea, Marc-Antoine Muret, Denys Lambin, and Adrianus Turnebus. The Senecan scholars included Erasmus, Calvin, Muret again, and Justus Lipsius. Full of Seneca were the very popular compilations of sayings by Crinitus, Rhodiginus, and Pedro de Mexia. Indeed it was mainly as a French Seneca that Lipsius and Etienne Pasquier admired Montaigne. In 1521, just after a young Franciscan named François Rabelais had become his friend by correspondence, the great Hellenist Guillaume Budé wrote a treatise on the contempt of fortuitous things. It is precisely this contempt on which even the optimistic Rabelais thirty years later based the gaiety of mind that was his ideal of Pantagruelism. In the closing years of the century this vein was stronger than ever. Montaigne's friend and disciple Pierre Charron was permeated with stoicism, his admirers Lipsius and Guillaume du Vair even more so. One authority sums it up by saying that Du Vair's early stoicism was not original because "it is like that of all the humanists."

But humanism is eclectic, and so was Montaigne. What he admired then and attacked later was not only stoicism, nor even stoicism plus Epicureanism; it was all dogmatic rational philosophy and its sweeping faith in the power of reason to guide our life well and happily. He had acquired the humanist's sense of being still in apprenticeship, and not to any one philosophic sect but to humanistic philosophy in general.

Whatever his other reasons for retiring—disappointment in the Parlement, weariness of unsuitable duties, desire or feeling of obligation to manage his home and estate—one reason was obviously that he wanted to meditate. What happened when he started he tells us in his chapter "Of Idleness" (I:8):

> The soul that has no fixed goal loses itself. . . .
>
> Lately when I retired to my home, determined so far as possible to bother about nothing except spending the little life I have left in rest and seclusion, it seemed to me I could do my mind no greater favor than to let it entertain itself in idleness and stay and settle in itself, which I hoped it might do more easily now, having become heavier and more mature with time. But I find . . . that, on the contrary, like

a runaway horse, it gives itself a hundred times more trouble than it took for others, and gives birth to so many chimeras and fantastic monsters, one after another, without order or purpose, that in order to contemplate their strangeness and foolishness at my pleasure, I have begun to put them in writing, hoping in time to make even my mind ashamed of them.

Montaigne may have had writing in mind from the first. His friend had written; he himself had published La Boétie's works and his own translation; he tells us later that he would as soon be father to a literary masterpiece as to a fine boy. At all events, his solitude needed occupation. A stirred and awakened soul, he says, is lost in itself unless it is given an object to act on. The occupation must not be troublesome or irritating; household management will not do for Montaigne, and even books and studies are dangerous, for they can absorb the reader beyond the limits of pleasure. But the books he likes are suitable: "books that are either pleasant and easy, which entertain me, or those that console me and counsel me to regulate my life and my death." Seneca's *Letters to Lucilius* and, after 1572, Plutarch's *Moral Essays* were his very favorites. But they were only two books out of a thousand; Montaigne's readings, especially in history and memoirs, where man is most frankly revealed, were vast.

To scribble notes in the margins or on the flyleaf of a book was not enough. His mind was wandering in search of a fixed goal; he must harness this runaway horse. Without a close friend, the need for some form of communication was great. And so he set out to write. But what was he to write? The full plan of the essay was not yet in his mind; he was trying his hand, to be sure, but the early chapters were only essays at writing essays. His main faculty already was his judgment; his main interests were political history, human nature, pain and death. So he gave us his judgments on these matters.

In the simplest and least personal of the early essays, Montaigne is little more than a political raconteur, hardly even a commentator. He compiles a string of anecdotes and draws a conclusion: "By Divers Means We Arrive at a Like End"; "Whether the Chief of a Besieged Place Should Go out to Parley"; "The Time of Parleys is Dangerous"; "Ceremony of the Interview of Kings"; and so on. Of this sort are essays I:5–7, 13, 15–17, 24, 34, 45. More interesting but still often meager of personality are the many (I:2–4, 8–11, 18, 21–23, 33, 36–38, 43–44, 46–48; II:2) that treat some aspect of human custom or behavior, usually to point up some paradox or inconsistency: "Sadness"; "Our Affections Go beyond Us"; "How the Soul Discharges Its Passions on False Objects when It Lacks the True"; "Idleness"; "Liars"; and the like. Most interesting are the chapters in which Montaigne grapples on paper with his greatest problem of the moment: how to prepare to meet pain and death worthily. Principal of these are "Constancy" (I:12); "That the Taste of Good and Evil Depends in Large Part on the Opinion We Have of Them" (I:14); "To Philosophize Is to Learn to Die" (I:20); "Solitude" (I:39); and "The Inconsistency of our Actions" (II:1).

Of all these early essays, some recall the compilations, the *leçons,* that were then so popular; some have a little of the flavor of Machiavelli's *Discourses;* others are a philosophical mosaic, but a mosaic still. Virtually all are rather short and mainly derivative. Montaigne himself said later that some of them smelled a little foreign. Here is material for his future conclusions—his skepticism, his sense of human complexity and vanity and of the problem of happy living—but the conclusions are not yet elaborated. Montaigne is on his way, but he has not gone far.

Actually, it is those conclusions which are most elaborated and apparently most his own that were to change most. These are his views on retirement and preparation for pain and death.

THE PROBLEM OF PAIN AND DEATH

Montaigne's early view of life was a rather Epicurean pessimism. "The wretchedness of our condition," he was to write, "makes us have less to desire than to fear. . . . That is why the sect of philosophy that set the greatest value on voluptuousness and raised it to its highest price still ranked it with mere freedom from pain. To have no ill is to have the happiest state of well-being that man can hope for."

Though he said that he had thus far lived reasonably happily, except for the loss of his friend, this was a great exception. Moreover, his other bereavements were to contribute their share to his pessimism. Fifteen years later the mere expressions that reminded him of his grief could still revive it: "My poor master! or, My great friend! Alas, my dear father! or, My good daughter!" In his gloomy apprehension, he looked for security in preparation, like the healthy young men he had seen carrying pills around to take in case of a cold. As the surest way to the negative contentment that seemed to him the best he could hope for, he sought not merely local retirement but withdrawal from all close human contacts:

> We should have wife, children, goods, and above all health, if we can; but not bind ourselves to them so strongly that our happiness depends on them. We must reserve a back shop all our own, entirely free, in which to establish our real liberty and our principal retreat and solitude . . . where to talk and laugh as if without wife, without children, and without possessions, without retinue and without servants, so that, when the time comes to lose them, it may be nothing new to us to do without them. . . .
>
> We have lived enough for others; let us live at least this remaining bit of life for ourselves. . . . It is no small matter to arrange our retirement securely. . . . Since God gives us leisure to make arrangements for moving out . . . let us pack our bags; let us take an early leave of the company. . . . We must untie these bonds that are so

powerful, and henceforth love this and that, but be wedded only to ourselves. That is to say, let the other things be ours, but not joined and glued to us so strongly that they cannot be detached without tearing off our skin and some part of our body as well. The greatest thing in the world is to know how to belong to oneself.

In the essay just quoted, "Of Solitude" (I:39), four principal menaces are listed: death, poverty, contempt, and disease. In another early essay (I:14) Montaigne mentions only three: death, poverty, and pain. Contempt did not disturb him seriously for very long, for he soon learned to know himself better than anyone else could know him and to rely on his laws and his court to judge himself. Poverty worried him somewhat for a while, but he knew that what we fear in it is pain. Pain and death are the great enemies, each with its claim to the first rank—death because it alone is inevitable, pain because it is what we fear even in death. Pain is more surely an evil, since death may by good fortune be painless; death is an evil more sure. Montaigne had seen both at close range. Death had been all around, and he thought and spoke of it most of all.

His thoughts on the subject are those of La Boétie. All the ideas he exchanged with his dying friend recur: that death is the test of our lives and our studies, the aim of philosophy and the proof that we have learned its lesson; that our own death should be an example that will encourage others to rise bravely above such accidents. Montaigne is not so much afraid of death—or pain—as apprehensive about how well he will be able to endure them.

The early essays are full of the problem. One of them (I:19) takes its title from Solon's famous pronouncement, "That Our Happiness Must not Be Judged until after Our Death." Solon was right, says Montaigne, since only in death can we tell what was mask and what was true philosophy in a man's life. Here alone there is no pretending: "That is why by this last act must be tried and tested all the other actions of our life. It is the master day, it is the day that is judge of all the others. . . . I refer until death the test of the fruit of my studies. We shall see then whether my reasonings come from my mouth or from my heart."

In "Judging the Death of Others" (II:13), Montaigne calls death man's most remarkable action. To judge it in another man, he says, we must know whether or not he was aware that he was dying. If he was not, or if he rushed to his end to get the inevitable over with, his heroism may well be overrated. The deaths of Cato and others like him, who studied and digested them, are hard but glorious in contrast; for death is "a meat which in truth must be swallowed without tasting unless a man's throat is frostshod." With obvious approval Montaigne tells Seneca's story of a stoic who explained to Marcellinus that "it is not much of a thing to live—your valets and the animals live—but it is a great thing to die honorably, wisely, and with constancy."

Montaigne's closest approach to death is the subject of "Practice" (II:6). Although probably written a little later than these others (in 1573 or 1574), this essay describes an event several years old about which Montaigne must have thought a good deal. Some time between 1567 and 1570 he was knocked unconscious for the first time in his life when thrown from his horse in a head-on collision with a larger horse and rider on a narrow path. He was unconscious for quite a time; he vomited much blood; when he came to, he thought he was dying. And the curious thing, he found, was that he did not want to come back to life and pain. His languor was rather sweet, like that of going off to sleep. His life seemed to be on his lips, and he tried to push it out. He had always thought that dying was something like this, less terrible than a well man might imagine. He had even argued the matter with La Boétie. Now he knew he was right, and this was a great comfort. For it proved that death may be painless; it showed that a sort of practice for it is possible; and, most important, it gave Montaigne a certain perspective. Before he had ever known sickness, he had imagined it as almost unendurable; when it came, it was not nearly so bad: "the force of my apprehension added almost half to the essence and truth of the thing."

But even with this reassurance, it is still a worried Montaigne who continues: "I hope that the same thing will happen to me with death, and that it is not worth the trouble I take with so many preparations that I set up and so many aids that I invoke and assemble to sustain the shock of it. But come what may, we cannot give ourselves too much advantage."

Apprendre is never closer to *apprehend* than in Montaigne's central chapter on death, "To Philosophize Is to Learn to Die" (I:20). Although generally stoical in tone, this is the mosaic of an eclectic humanist who draws on Pliny, Plutarch, and especially Lucretius, as well as on Cicero and Seneca. All sects agree, he says, that the main function of philosophy and reason is to teach us how to die. Death is universal, as pain and poverty are not. Ignorance is of no use, for it makes us suffer more when the time comes. We must practice death, get used to it, think about it constantly. The premeditation of death is the premeditation of liberty.

He himself, Montaigne continues, has always thought about it, read about it, talked about it: only recently, among his papers, someone found a note of his about something he wanted done after he died. He had written it a few miles from his house and in perfect health, but not confident of even reaching home alive. We must go on living normally, he insists, for we are born to act: for his own part, he hopes to die planting his cabbages, careless of death and of his imperfect garden. But first we must be prepared. Nature can make death easier by our illness or insensibility, by familiarizing us with the idea, and by giving us wise advice, if we will only listen. Leave life, she tells us, as you entered it, simply and unafraid; your death is a part of the order of things, an order you should not even wish to change.

To be sure, in an uneasy afterthought Montaigne asks why simple peasants are often the bravest of all at this last moment. But his answer now is that it must be the trappings of death we fear: if we strip off the mask, we shall find underneath the same enemy that a valet or a chambermaid has met unafraid. Presumably we can do better yet if we are prepared. For if we do not fear death, we have nothing to fear. This is the real freedom if we can achieve it.

With pain it is much the same for Montaigne. The great question here is the degree of truth in his chapter title, "That the Taste of Good and Evil Depends in Large Part on the Opinion We Have of Them" (I:14). It would be fine indeed if this were true, he says; unfortunately it does not seem to be. For pain is the real stuff, whose essence we truly and certainly know; our senses are the judges. It is what we fear in poverty and in death. We can hope for painless death, but hardly for painless pain. We must make our soul strong, clear, and patient, and avoid the cowardice that makes pain bolder. Things are not painful or difficult in themselves; it is our weakness and cowardice that make them so. Even common people have shown contempt for pain. Let us then gird ourselves and find a weapon against it. If worst comes to worst, we can always end it by suicide.

Altogether, the early essays are not gay. Life is mostly bad; its main facts are pain and death. For the problem of pain the only sure solution is death; for that of death, study and premeditation, tension and apprehension. In his tower, Montaigne is like a man besieged—not only by the things he fears but also by his own somber preparations for defense.

Like a man besieged or like a hunted man. In an early essay he tells the story of a noble Roman fugitive who had myriad narrow escapes from capture. Finally, after one of these, safe but exhausted, he called back to his pursuers to end his long agony. Montaigne remarks that "this is a rather extreme measure; yet I think it is still better to adopt it than to remain in continual fever over an accident that has no remedy." Even without his comment, the story would remind us of Montaigne.

THE HUMANIST'S SOLUTION

In such a situation a humanist may not merely relax and ignore the problem. He must call upon his studies, his philosophy, his ancient friends, to guide him. He must gird up his soul to the vigor and tension necessary for meeting the ills of life head on. But precisely why?

Montaigne seems to sense that this is the weakest point in his argument. Although he says that lack of preparation costs us too much in panic and torment at death, his explanation of the frequent bravery of simple people is not convincing, and he seems to know it; for he offers it tentatively and never repeats it. He knows that common people, whole nations, even cowards, can often perform the bravest actions even without study. He does not insist on the strictest possible regime of preparation, as do those who seek out privation. He says that we may use the body to help us if the soul is not strong enough alone; that all honorable assistance against the ills of life is not only permissible but even laudable.

To Montaigne at this stage of his development, however, preparation for trouble seems not only the way to freedom from fear but also, and above all, the duty of the humanist. It is his way of rising above the vulgar and, indeed, *the* thing that distinguishes the truly superior man.

Montaigne now fully shares the typical humanist attitude toward man's lot, which has been well defined as "an aristocratic optimism for the Sage, a pessimism as far as the Vulgar were concerned." The man he admires is the learned sage whom he calls "the man of understanding." It is he who can fight the fear to which the vulgar are prone; who has lost nothing so long as he has himself; in whose head Montaigne cannot imagine lodging the brutish nonchalance of not thinking about death. "I cannot believe," Montaigne writes, "that meanness of understanding can do more than vigor; or that the effects of reason cannot match the effects of habit." If reason sometimes fails to prepare us as well as ignorance, we are probably not using it properly. This is what he suggests when he tells for the first time a story he was to repeat in a later essay—how the philosopher Pyrrho encouraged his frightened fellow passengers in a terrible storm at sea by pointing to a tranquil pig that was literally in the same boat. "The intelligence," Montaigne asks, "that has been given us for our greatest good, shall we use it for our ruin, combating the plan of nature . . . ?"

Though something less than a glorious death might be sufficient, and though a glorious death sometimes seems not worth the price, still we must prepare for it. The opposite, the remedy of the vulgar, is gross blindness, brutish stupidity:

> What does it matter, you will tell me, how it happens, provided we do not worry about it? I am of that opinion; and in whatever way we can put ourselves in shelter from blows, even under a calf's skin, I am not the man to shrink from it. . . . But it is folly to expect to get there that way. They go, they come, they trot, they dance: of death no news. All that is fine. But when it comes, either to them, or to their wives, children, or friends, surprising them unprepared and defenseless, what torments, what cries, what frenzy! and what despair overwhelms them! . . . We must provide for this earlier; and this brutish nonchalance, even if it could lodge in the head of a man of understanding—which I consider entirely impossible—sells us its wares too dear.

Actually we should be grateful that pain exists, since it gives us our main chance for distinction. Men are much alike; but we have it in us to confine pain by endurance and to keep the soul if not the body on an even keel. If there were no pain, what credit would there be for valor, magnanimity, and resoluteness? If we do not have it to bear with triumphant calm, "how shall we acquire the advantage that we wish to have over the common herd?"

As a matter of fact, consistency as well as bravery sets the wise man apart from the *vulgaire*. Only the sage really exists, for only he is constant; the rest of mankind is in such a state of flux that it can hardly be said to exist at all. In "The Inconsistency of Our Actions" (II:1), Montaigne finds hardly a dozen ancients who have fashioned their lives, like Cato the Younger, to the certain and assured path that leads to wisdom. Most of us are mere puppets of appetite and circumstance: "Our ordinary practice is to follow the inclinations of our appetite, to the left, to the right, uphill and down, as the wind of circumstance carries us. We think of what we want only at the moment we want it, and we change like that animal which takes the color of the place you set it on. What we have just now planned, we presently change, and presently again we retrace our steps: nothing but oscillation and inconsistency. . . . We do not go; we are carried away, like floating objects. . . . Every day a new fancy, and our humors shift with the shifts in the weather." Indeed, our inconsistency makes us at times as different from ourselves as from others.

Greater than this difference, however, is that between the herd and the sage. Matching his own paradox and capping one of Plutarch's, Montaigne begins "The Inequality that Exists between Us" (I:42) by stating that "there is more distance from a given man to a given man than there is from a given man to a given animal." He anticipates the conclusion of the *Essays*—that even on the highest throne in the world a man is still seated on his own rear end—when he writes that we judge men mainly by their trappings, by the qualities least their own. A peasant and a king, in whom we see such disparity, "are different so to speak only in their breeches." Both are equally subject to all mortal ills; power and riches are no protection against pain and death. Behind the curtain, the emperor whose pomp dazzles us in public is nothing but a common man, perhaps viler than the least of his subjects. The base is not a part of the statue; the distinction between men is not social.

The real distinction is the one between the enlightened humanist and the common herd:

> Why in estimating a man do you estimate him all wrapped up in a package? . . . You must judge him by himself, not by his trappings. . . . Measure him without his stilts: let him put aside his riches and honors, let him present himself in his shirt. Has he a body fit for its functions, healthy, and blithe? What sort of soul has he? Is it beautiful, capable, and happily furnished with all its parts? Is it rich of its own riches, or of others'? has fortune nothing to do with it? If open-eyed it awaits the drawn swords; if it cares not whether its life expires by the mouth or the neck; if it is composed, equable, and content—that is what we must see, and thereby judge the extreme differences that are between us. Is he
>
> wise, and master of himself . . . ? [Horace]
>
> Such a man is five hundred fathoms above kingdoms and duchies: he is himself his own empire and riches; he lives satisfied, happy, and blithe. And to the man who has that, what is there left to want? . . . Compare with him the mob of our men, ignorant, stupid, and asleep, base, servile, full of fever and fright, unstable, and continually floating in the tempest of the diverse passions that push and drive them; depending entirely on others. There is more distance between them than between Heaven and earth.

Thus Montaigne's problem in the early *Essays* is not merely the human one of seeking happiness in liberation from fear but that of the humanist, who must rise above the common herd by his readiness to meet pain and death like a sage. Much as he admires Cato, his solution is not merely the stoic one, since all concur in it. It is the humanist's solution that seeks guidance in books, in the ancient sages, in self-mastery, in the power of the soul and of rational philosophy, to arm us against the ills of life. Montaigne cannot believe that reason and understanding, properly used, are not the best weapons of defense. The way he hopes to break his siege by apprehension is the humanist's way.

⸎ 3 ⸎

The Skeptical Revolt

1573-1576

THERE was a moment after the St. Bartholomew's Day Massacre when the Protestants seemed beaten, but it did not last. Coligny was dead, Navarre and Condé virtual prisoners; but in the masses the new faith showed its strength. Resistance was organized in the south; La Rochelle refused to admit the king's governor and held out bravely during a long siege; Nîmes and Montauban followed suit. When in 1573 the Polish electors chose Catherine de' Medici's second son, the duke of Anjou, as their king, she contentedly sent him away from the siege of La Rochelle to reign in Poland and granted freedom of worship to the three rebellious cities. A year later Anjou returned as Henry III to succeed his dead brother Charles IX. Discontent continued to grow, among Catholic nobles as well as Protestants. For a while, as Montaigne bitterly noted in his "Apology for Raymond Sebond," religion was more than ever the pretext for fighting, ambition and hatred the real motives. The new king's only surviving brother, the duke of Alençon, after stirring up trouble for several years, fled in 1575 to lead the united Protestants and malcontents. Soon Henry of Navarre also fled and resumed his former Reformed faith. The coalition forced on Henry III a peace treaty (1576) that rehabilitated the victims of St. Bartholomew's Day and gave the Protestants complete freedom of worship again. Immediately Duke Henri de Guise rallied intransigent Catholics all over

France into a League for the protection of Catholicism and the monarchy. Henry III, angry at his defeat, reluctantly recognized the League and became its head. The Catholic Estates General, assembled at Blois at the end of 1576, voted for the suppression of Protestantism by whatever means might be necessary. Though they changed their vote later, another war was on the way.

It was during these years that Montaigne was called on for what, as far as we know, was his first important task. According to De Thou's report of what Montaigne told him at the Estates General at Blois in 1588, Montaigne had tried to reconcile Navarre and Guise when they were both at court. In so doing he had learned that neither man really cared a bit for his professed religion; that Guise had tried to win Navarre's friendship and, that failing, had seen no recourse but to an enmity so violent that it could end only in the death of one or the other.

The only time when both men were at court was between 1572 and 1576. Montaigne tells us that he was cured of worry about money by a voyage of great expense four or five years after he became wealthy—in other words, presumably, in 1572 or 1573. And it is tempting to see an allusion to this event in another remark in the *Essays:* "I once tried to employ in the service of public dealings ideas and rules for living as crude, green, unpolished —or unpolluted—as they were born in me or derived from my education, and which I use, if not conveniently, at least surely, in private matters: a scholastic and novice virtue. I found them inept and dangerous for that."

Obviously Montaigne's attempt failed. Another time he was to succeed in dissuading a prince—probably Navarre—from rash vengeance, not by book-learned morality but by diversion. It is possible, though conjectural, that he had learned his lesson with Navarre and Guise earlier, and that it had helped teach him to distrust dogmatic systems of theoretical morality.

Not much else is known of Montaigne's life in these four years.

He was involved in certain legal disputes over successions. Another daughter was born and shortly died. The governor of Bordeaux sent him to the duke of Montpensier, commander of the royal army in the region, to ask his will concerning a local dispute over a command, and Montaigne brought back a letter from the duke to the Parlement which was read to the Grand'Chambre and then further explained by its bearer. He tells us that he was often away from home but gives no details. Much of his time he spent in his tower, on his *Essays*. More and more he found himself dissatisfied with stoical humanism; finally he rejected it entirely.

GROWING DISSATISFACTION

Often in the late years of his life, Montaigne still spoke of stoical humanism as an ideal higher than his own. Many of his readers have taken him rather literally. "He is a weak man who falls in love with the strong," writes a recent critic. "Stoicism . . . set to vibrating in him strings all the more sensitive in that they were made up of impotence and flabbiness."

Actually, the notion that in abandoning stoical humanism Montaigne gave up what he considered best is false. What happened was that he came to regard the attitude he had formerly admired as unfit for himself, fit at best only for a few, unsound for mankind in general. If anything was an aberration in his development, it was not his flight from stoical humanism but his attraction to it. It was probably a necessary stage. But in leaving it, he became less the survivor of La Boétie and more Michel de Montaigne.

Even in his years of apprehension he was not a thoroughgoing sage or even an apprentice. Heroism was only a means to his constant end of happiness; he did not ask miracles of himself; he would, as he said, take to a calf's skin for shelter, if only that would work. His wise man whom he sets above kingdoms is fit for enjoyment as well as endurance.

Central in the movement of Montaigne's thought between 1573

and 1576 is his progressive critique of stoical humanism. He soon saw that he was too earthy for it to fit him. "Crawling on the slime of the earth," he writes, "I do not fail to note, even in the clouds, the loftiness of certain heroic souls." His statement shows unconcern as well as admiration. His feeling is not one of inferiority but of incompatibility. To feel different, for Montaigne, was not to feel, like a romantic, necessarily superior; nor yet was it to feel inferior. For intention, he found, we are responsible, but results are often beyond our powers.

He was already becoming aware of a certain immutability in human nature. Some things, he felt, we simply cannot digest, and those things we cannot use. Our ideals as well as our ideas are of no use to us unless they are our very own: "We know how to say: 'Cicero says thus; that is Plato's opinion; these are Aristotle's very words.' But we, what do we say ourselves? what is our opinion? how do we judge? A parrot would easily do as much. . . . What good is it to us to have our belly full of meat, if it is not digested? if it is not transformed into us? if it does not augment and fortify us? . . . Even if we could be learned with others' learning, at least wise we cannot be except with our own wisdom."

For all his variability and change, by temperament and by judgment Montaigne was fundamentally static rather than kinetic, an accepter rather than a reformer. He sought harmony within, not conflict. By the early 1570s, he had begun to base his self-acceptance on the conviction that it is impossible for us even to want to change much. "It is by a similar vanity," he writes, "that we wish to be something other than what we are. The fruit of such a desire does not affect us, because it contradicts and entangles itself in itself. He who wishes to be made from a man into an angel, he does nothing for himself. For since he will no longer exist, he will no longer have the wherewithal to rejoice in this improvement and feel it."

The example of change he gives is drastic; it is drastic change, now as later, that he denies we can make. Already his chapter "Of Pedantry" (I:25), like the later chapter on education (I:26) and indeed the whole Third Book, shows his belief that some amelioration is possible. But it should concentrate on essentials, whereas stoicism seems to consider all vices as equal. And it must be so to speak in our own terms, in terms of the natural lines of growth that are possible for us. If we try too hard, we can do nothing. As proof that our will is not omnipotent, Montaigne likes to point to the male member, which may lie down on the job, as it were, if we are too eager for it not to. And the same thing is true, he finds, of the soul in general: "I know by very personal and ordinary experience that natural condition that cannot endure a vehement premeditation. . . . The worry about doing well, and that tension of the soul that is too strained and too tightened in its enterprise, racks it and confuses it."

Since stoical humanism vainly ignores or tries to suppress this fundamental contrariness of man, Montaigne soon grew very dubious of its value. Ignorance and habit, he noted, have done better for ordinary people than study and effort for the philosophers. As for the true and successful sages, they are rare indeed. More and more he came to feel that his earlier ideal, impractical as well as unsound, was therefore dubious and questionable—for even virtue must be sociable and usable.

Consistency was one of the main values that Montaigne had sought in stoical humanism, and he began to suspect that it was not there. At least, he had not found it in precisely what he had most admired in that school. Since man cannot remain constantly on such a high level, the greatest deeds of the greatest heroes are inconsistencies and aberrations:

> Surely one must confess that in those souls there is some alteration and some frenzy, however holy it be.
>
> When we come to these stoical sallies: "I would rather be insane than voluptuous" . . . when Sextius tells us that he would rather

be pierced through by pain than by sensual pleasure; when Epicurus . . . cheerfully defies ills and, scorning the less severe pains . . . invokes and wishes for pains strong and poignant . . . who does not judge that those are sallies of a courage flung out of its abode? Our soul from its seat could not reach so high. It must leave it and rise, and, taking the bit in its teeth, ravish and carry away its man so far that afterward he is himself astonished at his action.

Inconsistent in its lofty flights, the philosophy of tension is histrionic and comic at other times. Even in one of his earliest essays Montaigne had shown his awareness of this when he told, for the first time, one of his favorite stories in this vein. Posidonius was suffering acutely from a painful illness when a friend came to visit him and apologized for coming at a bad time. Posidonius replied that pain could not stop him from talking about his contempt for it. But his trouble pressed him hard, and he cried out: "Do your worst, pain, still I will not admit that you are an evil." Montaigne's comment is derisive: "This story that they make so much of, what has it to do with contempt for pain? He is only arguing about the word; and meanwhile, if these stings do not move him, why does he break off his conversation for them? Why does he think he is doing a lot by not calling it an evil?"

The austerity of traditional humanism is both immoderate and negative. It is a philosophy of death, and Montaigne had begun to rally to the defense of life. The sage, he tells us, may change his pace as a concession to human passions; he need not, like some, "plant himself like an immobile and impassible colossus." Seneca's advice to Lucilius, to quit his life of pomp and ceremony or else quit life itself, sounds, says Montaigne, like "stoical harshness" but is actually borrowed from Epicurus' advice to Idomeneus; it is in marked contrast with Christian moderation.

Humanistic philosophy is not only immoderate but immodest. It errs morally as well as intellectually in failing to recognize the inherent weakness of man. Even its sage cannot live up to what it claims that man can do. Its adherents try to be superhuman, but they are merely inhuman. Nature is far too strong for them. In "Drunkenness" (II:2), the silly question whether wine can overpower the soul of the sage leads Montaigne to speak his mind:

> Out of a thousand, there is not one [soul] that is straight and composed at any moment of its life; and it might be doubted whether according to its natural condition it can ever be so. But as for combining this with constancy, that is the soul's ultimate perfection; I mean even if nothing should jar it. . . . Let him be as wise as he please, after all he is a man: what is there more vulnerable, more wretched and more null? Wisdom does not overcome our natural conditions. He must blink his eyes at the blow that threatens him; he must shudder if you plant him on the edge of a precipice. He pales with fear, he reddens with shame; he moans at the colic. . . . Enough for him to curb and moderate his inclinations; for to do away with them is not in him.

This presumption and immoderation makes stoical humanism also un-Christian. In "Custom of the Island of Cea" (II:3), Montaigne contrasts its approval of suicide with Christian disapproval; and though he does not clearly state his position, it seems to be the latter. He starts with a number of quotations giving the view that we have seen in his early essays. Death is the ultimate solution for unbearable pains or griefs; we cannot complain of life when the way out is open. He seems to sympathize with this view, and returns to it with more examples after presenting its opposite.

Meanwhile, however, he has pointed out the other side of the picture. Christianity in particular does not allow suicide, saying that God alone, who put us here, has the right to take us away. If Montaigne was a sincere Christian, as most of the evidence suggests, this is a telling point. At the very least it is a clear recognition of the complete antagonism on this central issue between stoical humanism and Christianity.

Moreover, Montaigne goes on—and he seems to be speaking for himself—there is something cowardly and unnatural about suicide and the doctrine that approves it. To hide in a tomb is still to hide: it is braver to endure. To reject life is the action of a mind diseased: "The opinion that disdains our life is ridiculous in us. For after all it is our being, it is our all. Things that have a nobler and richer being can accuse ours; but it is unnatural that we despise ourselves and care nothing about ourselves; it is a malady peculiar to us, and which is seen in no other creature, to hate and combat oneself." Thus this humanistic doctrine is not only un-Christian but unnatural.

For Montaigne these two things are much the same. The main weakness of his Christianity is an almost complete identification of the order of nature with the order of God. He seeks God less in the Bible than in his creation, less through revelation than through reason. For him what is Christian may be natural or supernatural; what is natural is nearly always Christian.

Hence any virtue that is not moderate and natural is a failure, in Montaigne's eyes, both by human and by Christian standards. In the essay "Of Moderation" (I:30), difficult to date but probably of this period, he makes this clear when he writes:

> As if our touch were contagious, we corrupt by our handling the things which of themselves are fair and good. We can seize virtue in such a way that it will thereby become vicious, as happens when we embrace it with too sharp and violent a desire. Those who say that there is never excess in virtue, since it is no longer virtue if there is excess in it, are playing with the subtlety of words. . . . One can both love virtue too much and behave immoderately in a just and virtuous action. The divine saying can be adapted to this angle: "Be not wiser than you should, but be soberly wise."

For excessive austerity of the stoical type is a concoction all man's own, one of his sorriest attempts to outdo nature. Our misery is all of our own making: "To speak in dead earnest, is not man a miserable animal? Hardly is it in his power, by his natural condition, to enjoy a single entire and pure pleasure, and still he labors to cut it down by reason. He is not wretched enough if he does not augment his misery by art and by study."

Montaigne attacks stoical humanism for refusing to recognize not only the limitations that nature imposes on us but also her generous gifts. He is just beginning to see nature as mainly benign. He has not yet gone far. Socrates, the one sage who worshiped and personified this benignity of nature, is mentioned only three times, and without comment, before 1576; later his name will appear nearly a hundred times, and with Montaigne's warmest praise. But Montaigne notes nature's kindness to all creatures who are closest to her and depend on her most—animals, savages, beggars, common folk. These are not precisely the *vulgaire* of the earliest essays, but they belong in that group and certainly not among the sages. Simple, unopinionated, and relaxed, following their inclinations, they might well be called nature's *vulgaire*. Compared with these trustful children of nature, the humanist sages are foolish prodigals. Their dogmatic philosophy is unsound, impractical, inconsistent, immoderate, comically presumptuous, un-Christian, and unnatural. In the years before the "Apology for Raymond Sebond" these points have been clearly sketched. In that chapter they will be fully and happily developed into a sweeping critique of all dogmatic philosophy.

REVOLT: THE "APOLOGY"

Three times as long as the next-longest essay, the "Apology for Raymond Sebond" makes up almost one sixth of Montaigne's entire book. Centrally located as well as huge, embodying the famous motto "What do I know?" it has long been accepted as the center of his thought. It has seemed a little less important, because less typical of his final ideas, to most scholars of the present century. However, it retains its interest as the fullest expression of his skepticism and as one of the decisive steps in his evolution.

It has meant many things to its many readers. Rousseau drew on it for his critique of civilization. Freethinkers of the seventeenth and eighteenth centuries used it as an arsenal of weapons against authoritarian religion. Pascal and many readers since have been struck mainly by its fideism, or divorce of faith and reason in matters of religion to the advantage of the former. For Villey it expresses Montaigne's skeptical crisis, brought on around 1576 by his reading Sextus Empiricus' *Outlines of Pyrrhonism,* which released him from his "stoical" attitude to his freer "Epicurean" one. Because Montaigne's reasoning draws blood from Sebond as well as from his critics, some of his most brilliant readers, such as Sainte-Beuve and Gide, have interpreted the essay as a covert but thorough undermining of Christianity and all dogmatic religion.

Skeptical and fideistic though it is, it is probably innocent of antireligious malice. Perfidy is a thing that Montaigne hated and scorned. Most of the arguments for its treachery assume that the apparent betrayal of Sebond is a real one that betrays Christianity as well. There is much evidence against this assumption. Montaigne's fideism was acceptable to the Church of his time and was not even mentioned by the papal censors; he could not be expected to know that a hundred years later it would be unorthodox and the *Essays* placed on the Index (1676). Nor should he be mistrusted because later admirers applied his critique of philosophy and of other religions to Catholicism, which he had set above the reach of reason. His treatment of Sebond is disconcerting, but it smacks far more of unconcern than of betrayal. Though he had translated him, he had never wholly admired him; and now he seems to be genuinely trying to speak well of a weak thinker whom some admire, who means well, and who may be useful. It is likely that most of the essay was written simply as an attack on human reason and presumption, and only later arranged as an "Apology for Raymond Sebond" at the request of Margaret of Valois.

The proportions of the essay show how little Sebond has to do with it. Since Montaigne says that he has been asked to defend his man against two groups of objectors, the reader expects an introduction, two fairly equal main parts, and a conclusion. But the defensive part is almost negligible; the counterattack against the second group of critics fills over nine tenths of the whole essay; the beginning and conclusion of the essay bear on the counterattack alone. Obviously this is the important part, to which the rest is merely introduction and setting.

Montaigne makes no formal divisions within the "Apology," but he frequently tells us where we are going and where we have been. Viewed in its own terms, the chapter appears as a short introduction in defense of Sebond (22 pages in Villey's 1930–31 edition) and as a counterattack on the vanity of man and his knowledge without God (310 pages). The introduction (pages 212–34) opens with a keynote statement that knowledge is useful but overrated, continues with a short account of Sebond and his book and of Montaigne's connection with them, and then comes to the two main objections to Sebond. With the first, which is that human reason should not be used to try to prove religious truth, Montaigne deals briefly and obliquely, for the very good reason that he evidently shares it. All he can say for Sebond on this score is that the Christianity of the men of his time is so bad that they obviously receive it only by human means; in which case there may be a use for Sebond, whose work is as good as any of its kind. The second objection is that Sebond's reasons are not good reasons, that his critics can show him up. After three pages on the objectors and in Sebond's defense, Montaigne happily rolls up his sleeves and starts to work on these presumptuous fools.

In the long counterattack (pages 234–544) seven main parts may be distinguished, or five plus an introduction and a conclusion. Pointing to presumption as our worst and most inherent malady, Montaigne takes up the challenge of the rationalists by inviting us to consider man without divine aid: what he can do and know without the divine knowledge and grace that are his sole strength and honor and the foundation of his whole being.

Except as the son of God made in God's image, what claim has he to be the center of the universe, lord of creation? In the first main part (239–306) Montaigne shows that man without God is neither abler nor less able than the animals; in his second part (306–34), that even if man has knowledge and reason, these make him neither happier nor better. The long third part (334–447) is a demonstration of human ignorance. The most learned of men, the philosophers, especially the dogmatists, all disagree even on the most essential things: God, the human soul, the human body. Only the Pyrrhonists are wise, who claim that they are still in search of the truth.

Montaigne now pauses in his short fourth part (pages 447–51) to warn the noble lady for whom the essay is written to use what follows only as a last resort. For the long fifth part (pages 451–544) is an attempt to prove that man not only does not know anything, but cannot. His intelligence, like himself, is unstable and ever-changing, out of contact with perfect and absolute truth. His senses, the beginning and the end of his knowledge, are incapable of certainty, probably deficient, deceiving the soul and deceived by it in turn. Because he is constantly changing, never being but only becoming, man cannot know other things, which are also changing. Nor can he know unchanging God, for flux has no knowledge of being. Hence Montaigne's double conclusion: man is a wretched thing unless he rises above humanity; he can do so only by the grace of God.

Skepticism is certainly one of the major themes of this complex essay; but its importance is often overrated. Montaigne was a skeptic before and after; any notion of a "skeptical crisis" seems excessive. The "Apology" is simply the fullest expression of his reasons for doubt, written at a time when Sextus Empiricus has just made him aware of the full dialectical strength of the Pyrrhonist position. This skepticism is not an end in itself but a means to an end, a way of confounding the arrogant dogmatists. Montaigne's account of the Pyrrhonist method well describes his own here—and often elsewhere: "They do not fear contradiction in their discussion. When they say that heavy things go down, they would be very sorry to have anyone take their word for it; and they seek to be contradicted, so as to create doubt and suspension of judgment, which is their goal. They advance their propositions only to combat those that they think we believe in."

Montaigne's skepticism here is an intellectual game, the game of the paradox, in which he delights. He was to remark once later that "I often risk mental sallies that I mistrust." Now, in much of the "Apology," he is playful. Either uncritically or with tongue in cheek, he throws any argument, good or bad, at his equally uncritical adversaries. Often this trait leads him into real inconsistencies. For example, after arguing that we cannot know what is likely (*vraisemblable*—like truth) if we do not know what is true, he does not hesitate to point out later that Pyrrhonism is a critique of experience by reason, in which "they demonstrate that we do not move, that we do not speak, that there is no weight or heat, with the same force and subtlety of arguments with which we prove the most likely (*vraisemblables*) things."

Furthermore, Pyrrhonism is set up as a model in moral as well as intellectual matters. Followers of nature, not of art, moderates and not extremists, the Pyrrhonists are above all simple and human. Elsewhere Montaigne accepts the stories of their eccentricities; but here he will not:

As for the actions of life, they are of the common fashion in that. They lend and accommodate themselves to natural inclinations, to the impulsion and constraint of passions, to the constitutions of laws and customs, and to the tradition of the arts. They let their common actions be guided by those things without any taking sides or judgment. Which is why I cannot very well reconcile with this principle what Laertius says about the life of Pyrrho. . . . He did not want to make himself a stump or a stone: he wanted to make himself a living man, thinking and reasoning, enjoying all natural pleasures and comforts, employing and using all his bodily and spiritual faculties. The fantastic, imaginary, false privileges that man has usurped, of judging, knowing, ordering, establishing, he honestly renounced and gave up.

All this is obviously something more than intellectual skepticism. With respect to the unfolding of Montaigne's thought, the most important aspect of the "Apology" is the critique of the moral code of all dogmatic rational philosophy, especially of the rigoristic type.

In a sense the whole essay is not about the critics of Sebond, who are alluded to rarely and vaguely, but about the ancient dogmatic philosophers and their follies. Montaigne's man without divine grace or knowledge, who is hard to imagine theologically, seems to be simply the philosophers' man—man as the ancients saw him or had reason to see him. It is mere man—man as he would be if God had not chosen him for salvation, made him in his own image, and redeemed him with the blood of his Son—who struts comically through the pages of the ancients and of Montaigne's longest chapter.

Montaigne begins his counterattack by pointing out that if man would accept the Christian truth that our wisdom is folly before God, all this argument would be unnecessary. But he is too vain:

> Presumption is our natural and original malady. The most vulnerable and frail of all creatures is man, and at the same time, says Pliny, the most arrogant. He feels and sees himself lodged here, amid the mire and dung of the world . . . and in his imagination he goes planting himself above the circle of the moon and bringing the sky down beneath his feet. It is by the vanity of this same imagination that he equals himself to God, that he attributes to himself divine characteristics, that he picks himself out and separates himself from the horde of other creatures.

The means Montaigne finds fittest to beat down the frenzy of the rationalists, the program of his whole counterattack, is: "To crush and trample underfoot human arrogance and pride; to make them [the rationalists] feel the inanity, the vanity and nothingness of man; to wrest from their hands the puny weapons of their reason; to make them bow their heads and bite the ground beneath the authority and reverence of divine majesty."

His first step is to show, by countless tall tales, that we are no cleverer, no happier, and no better than the animals. We are neither spoiled nor neglected, neither above nor below the rest. In our pride we have left nature's way, and we are the worse for it. We are all feeble, calamitous, and miserable. Our artifice is a waste of time: "it is a marvel how little nature needs to be content."

Even if we do have a faculty of reason that the other creatures lack, it is not worth the price we set on it. Cicero talks about the man of learning as if he were God almighty; but a thousand village women have lived better and happier lives than he. Even "my Seneca" claims that he owes life to God, but the good life to himself. Nothing is commoner than this absurd temerity. "There is not one of us who is so offended to see himself compared to God as he is to see himself brought down to the rank of the other animals: so much more jealous are we of our own interest than of that of our creator. But we must tread this stupid vanity underfoot. . . . Man . . . must be stripped right down to his shirt."

For all their talk of the value of wisdom, the philosophers give themselves away when they say that Heraclitus with the gout and Pherecydes with lice would have done well, if they could, to exchange their wisdom for health. Worse yet, they say that if Circe had given Ulysses the choice of becoming a witless human or a virtuous stoical sage of an animal, he should have chosen to be the former. Thus even they admit that our only real advantage is our alleged beauty, and that this is greater than the wisdom of the sage.

What use, Montaigne asks, is reason to our happiness? What good did it do Varro and Aristotle to know so much? "Did it exempt them from human discomforts? . . . Did they derive from logic some consolation for the gout? For knowing how this humor lodges in the joints, did they feel it less? Were they reconciled to death for knowing that some nations rejoice in it . . . ?" Here is Posidonius again, refusing to call pain pain: "nothing but wind and words." Here are Pyrrho and the pig again, but with a different moral. Montaigne's comment earlier had been that we must use our reason better. Now he finds that reason is of no use: "But even if knowledge actually did, as they say, blunt and lessen something of the stings of pain and of the keenness of the misfortunes that pursue us, what does it do but what ignorance does much more purely and more evidently? . . . Philosophy, at the end of her precepts, sends us back to the examples of an athlete or a muleteer."

Since we have less to hope for than to fear in life, simplicity does very well for us if it leads to our having no pain. Reason can be an actual obstacle to happiness. For apprehension, which not long before Montaigne had thought necessary, now seems to do more harm than good:

> When real evils fail us, knowledge lends us hers. . . . Compare the life of a man enslaved to such imaginings with that of a plowman letting himself follow his natural appetites, measuring things only by the present taste of them, without knowledge and without prognostication, and who has pain only when he has it. Whereas the other often has the stone in his soul before he has it in his loins. As if he were not in time enough to suffer the pain when he is in it, he anticipates it in imagination and runs to meet it.

Knowledge itself admits that ignorance is bliss by telling us in affliction to think of other things, to forget the ugly present for the happier past. This is an unworthy trick, and not even a good one: what good is it to a man with a burning fever to remember the sweetness of Greek wine? Furthermore, the psychology of the philosophers is again unsound. We do not have the power of forgetting at will. "For memory sets before us, not what we choose, but what it pleases. Indeed there is nothing that imprints a thing so vividly on our memory as the desire to forget it." Even suicide, which philosophy allows as a last resort, is a confession of impotence, an appeal not to reason but to insensibility and nonexistence.

Completely useless for our happiness and often harmful to it, rational philosophy is equally powerless to make us good. "As by simplicity life becomes pleasanter," Montaigne continues, "so also does it become better and more innocent, as I was starting to say a while back. The simple and ignorant, says Saint Paul, raise themselves to heaven, and take possession of it; and we, with all our learning, plunge into the infernal abyss." The nations of the new world live better without magistrates or laws than ours that are overrun with them. Simplicity, humility, obedience, and amenability, the principal Christian and social virtues, are usually found in company with ignorance.

Christians have better reason than others to know the danger of the *libido sciendi.* The urge to grow in wisdom and knowledge was the first downfall of the human race. As the Bible often makes clear, pride is ever our undoing. It is out of pride that we try to define and limit God, when our concepts do not even apply to him.

> It is for God alone to interpret his works and to know himself. . . . Our faith is not of our own acquiring, it is a pure present of another's liberality. It is not by reasoning or by our understanding that we have received our religion; it is by external authority and command. The weakness of our judgment helps us more in this than its strength, and our blindness more than our clearsightedness. It is by the mediation of our ignorance more than of our knowledge that we are learned with that divine learning. . . . Let us bring to it nothing of our own but obedience and submission.

Having shown the dangers of thinking that we have knowledge, Montaigne turns, for the remainder of the essay, to the question whether in fact we have true knowledge, or can have it.

"Yet must I see at last," he writes, "whether it is in the power of man to find what he seeks, and whether that quest that he has been making for so many centuries has enriched him with any new power and any solid truth." It is the second question that he tackles first.

Most of his long demonstration of the follies of philosophy is not central to our argument here; human ignorance was no new theme to him, though he had never dwelt on it so extensively. What is striking is the repudiation of the humanist sage, who is the butt of the comedy. It would be too easy, says Montaigne, to use the stupidities of the unthinking herd to make a fool of man:

> I wish to take man in his highest estate. Let us consider him in that small number of excellent and select men who, having been endowed with fine and particular natural ability, have further strengthened and sharpened it by care, by study, and by art, and have raised it to the highest pitch that it can attain. They have fashioned their soul to all directions and all angles, supported and propped it with all the outside assistance that was fit for it, and enriched and adorned it with all they could borrow, for its advantage, from the inside and the outside of the world; it is in them that the utmost height of human nature is found. . . . I shall take into account only these people. . . . The infirmities and defects that we shall find in this assembly the world may well boldly acknowledge as its own.

Philosophers, he goes on, fall into three classes according to their respective claims: that they have found the truth; that it cannot be found; or that they are still looking for it. The worst of these are the dogmatists—peripatetics, Epicureans, stoics, and the like. Clitomachus, Carneades, and the academics, who decided that man could not know truth, are better. But the only wise philosophers are those who have confessed their ignorance and still gone on searching. Among them is Socrates, whom Montaigne now describes, for the first time, as "the wisest man that ever was." Most of them are the skeptics or epechists who follow Pyrrho. They use their reason to inquire and debate but reserve all final judgment; their philosophy is a perpetual confession of ignorance. They behave simply, sociably, and normally, for they are not so presumptuous as to think they know better.

The most plausible of human philosophies, theirs is also the ideal preparation for Christianity: "It presents man naked and empty, acknowledging his natural weakness, fit to receive from above some outside power; stripped of human knowledge, and all the more apt to lodge divine instruction and belief; not setting up dogma, and consequently free from the vain and irreligious opinions introduced by the other sects. 'Receive things thankfully,' says Ecclesiastes, 'in the aspect and taste that they are offered to thee, from day to day; the rest is beyond thy knowledge.'"

Most of the dogmatists, Montaigne argues, were really skeptics at heart but wanted to show how far they had gone in pursuit of truth. Many were willfully obscure. They despised each other's fields of inquiry. Socrates and Seneca despised all studies except that of morals and life. Many of them were like Democritus, who found a flavor of honey in some figs and was happily theorizing about the nature of the soil that produced them, when his maid spoiled his fun by telling him that the jar they were in had held honey. Whereat Democritus scolded her and went on theorizing anyway.

It is impossible, Montaigne goes on, to explain some of their follies except as playing with ideas. Their presumption in speculating about God cannot be understood otherwise. "For what is there, for example, more vain than to try to regulate God and the world by our capacity and our laws?" The best form of worship that Saint Paul found in Athens was that of an unknown God. Of all the merely human opinions held by the ancients about God, the wisest was that which regarded him as "an incomprehensible power, origin and preserver of all things, all goodness, all perfection, accepting and taking in good part the honor and reverence that human beings rendered him, under whatever aspect and in whatever manner it might be."

Here, indeed, as elsewhere, "man can be only what he is, and imagine only within his reach." God has not let us into His secrets. When we try to argue what He can or cannot do, we are utterly out of our element. This is our ultimate presumption and folly. In this respect the Protestants are the worst of the Christians, the stoics among the worst of the pagans; but none of us are innocent. As soon as human reason leaves the beaten path of the Church, it is lost in "that vast, troubled, and undulating sea of human opinions."

In our knowledge of ourselves we are no better off. If we had any knowledge, that would be it. The all-knowing people who criticize Sebond know nothing about themselves, not even about how spirit works on body. Blind worshipers of Aristotle, they accept the old mistakes and build on them uncritically. Allow their first principles, and you are at their mercy; challenge them, and they will not even argue with such a skeptic. Now, God alone can have revealed first principles. Nothing else is certain, not even common sense, which the philosophers have so ingeniously ruined for themselves. Reason, they tell us, is the touchstone; but reason knows nothing certain, not even of itself or of the soul. Here again the philosophers give us nothing but nonsense, Plato and Aristotle, stoics and Epicureans alike. They will not see the implications of the soul's helplessness against wine, fever, or hydrophobia. Nor do we know any more about the body than about the soul: the various theories of reproduction are a quick and decisive proof. In short, man knows no more of himself than he does of God, and since he does not know himself, he knows nothing.

Montaigne now inserts a warning against going farther. It is better to stay on the beaten path if possible, he says; our mind is dangerously erratic, and we should not give up our weapons too readily in order to make our opponent lose his. But if one of these new doctors presses you too hard, at the peril of your salvation and his, here is the fencer's trick you need, the proof that our reason is naturally and intrinsically impotent.

Some say that even if we cannot know what is true, we may still know what is probable. This Montaigne denies on the ground that if we do not know truth we cannot know what resembles it. "Either we can judge absolutely or we absolutely cannot." Since no two people agree perfectly on any matter of sense or knowledge, it is obvious that our perception is also a distortion.

We can see the insecurity of our judgment by its constant variations. Again and again we have embraced some notion with all our heart and soul, only to change our minds about it soon after. Our condition is one of flux; we must learn its lesson. Body and soul, we are subject to so many conditions, vicissitudes, and changes, that "we can hardly find a single hour of our life when our judgment is in its proper seat." If we know nothing else, at least we must know that our very nature makes us incapable of attaining absolute truth except by outside help. "At least we must become wise at our own expense."

The soul is affected not only by the passions of the body but also, and more so, by its own. Most of the finest deeds depend on them: "no eminent and lusty virtue is without some unruly agitation." These passions make us see things in a different way than when we are calm. But which is the true way? Pyrrho does not know.

Change is the rule of the race as well as of the individual. When people tell him that the ancients did not know how to navigate and got where they wanted by luck and for the wrong reasons, Montaigne answers that he prefers to be guided by facts and results rather than by reason. It would have been Pyrrhonizing a thousand years before to believe in the existence of countries that have since been discovered. We must learn to be this sort of

Pyrrhonists. The best products of our understanding—laws, customs, beliefs, opinions of virtue and vice, interpretations—are all subject to the laws of nature and of flux: they are born, change, and die, like ourselves and like all creatures. But "truth must have one face, the same and universal." It cannot be found in these changing ideas of ours.

Our senses are the greatest proof of our ignorance. They are our last resort: "Knowledge begins through them and is resolved into them." If we cannot be sure of their testimony we can be sure of nothing. And we cannot. We probably do not have all the senses we need: we have five which are often in conflict, and we probably need eight or ten to have true knowledge. The Epicureans, desperately and absurdly, say that we must believe the senses anyway, else we have no knowledge. Put this together, Montaigne will add later, with the stoics' claim that the senses are utterly untrustworthy, and "we shall conclude, at the expense of these two great dogmatic sects, that there is no knowledge."

The senses have dominion over us and make fools of us if we challenge them. "The sense of touch . . . overthrows . . . all those beautiful stoical resolutions and compels the man to cry out at his stomach who has established with all resoluteness this doctrine in his soul, that the colic, like every other malady and pain, is an indifferent thing, not having the power to reduce at all the sovereign happiness and felicity in which the sage is lodged by his virtue." The philosopher suspended in a metal net between the towers of Notre Dame is terrified, for all his philosophy. Our natural condition is too strong.

Probably deficient, deceiving the soul, the senses are deceived by it in turn. Its passions affect our simplest perceptions. When we disagree with the animals, shall we trust our senses or theirs? Who is to say? We need to agree with the animals, and we do not; we need to agree with ourselves, and we cannot. When are we right, when wrong? We do not know. We need a judge, but a judge exempt from all influencing conditions, such a judge as never was. Or we need a judicatory instrument, which in turn must be verified, and the verifier verified, and so *ad infinitum.*

Worst of all, the soul has no direct contact with externals. The senses offer it not the object but only the impact it makes on them. This is not the same thing as the object, and we simply cannot be sure whether or not the two are alike.

Finally, no certain judgment of things can be in us when both we and they are constantly changing. Flux cannot truly know flux. Nor can flux have communication with being. Following Plutarch almost word for word, Montaigne develops this theme in some detail. God alone is, God alone does not change, God alone can know absolute truth which like him is eternal and unchanging. Even if truth could lodge in us, by that very fact it would immediately and automatically lose its eternal and absolute quality. To this "religious conclusion" of one pagan he adds the remark of another, Seneca: "O what a vile and abject thing is man, if he does not raise himself above humanity!"

Thus the essay returns in conclusion to the lofty aspiration of stoical humanism. And Montaigne's comment, the end of the "Apology" in its original form, is that this aspiration is pointless:

> There is no truer saying in all his stoical school than that one. But to make the handful bigger than the hand, the armful bigger than the arm, and to hope to straddle more than the reach of our legs, is impossible and unnatural. Nor can man raise himself above himself and humanity; for he can see only with his own eyes, and seize only with his own grasp. He will rise, if God lends him his hand; he will rise by abandoning and renouncing his own means, and letting himself be raised and uplifted by divine grace; but not otherwise.

Here as often elsewhere the "Apology" is not so much an intellectual inquest into reason and faith as a treatment of the moral question: What can man do to make himself better? On this question depends the moral ideal—for Montaigne is convinced that an attainable ideal is a condition of improvement.

The ideal of stoical humanism, that man should raise himself by his bootstraps above humanity, is unattainable and therefore futile. It not only fails on the purely human level but leaves us in no position to hope for divine help. Ethically and intellectually, Pyrrhonism is sounder—ethically for setting up an attainable ideal, intellectually for making us a blank page on which God may write if he will; and therefore ethically again for practicing humility and avoiding man's pet vice, presumption.

When Montaigne entered the "Apology," he had for some time been considering critically the moral ideal that had drawn him earlier and that La Boétie had revered. By the end of the essay he had done with it. Stoical humanism was not for him, nor did he think it was for others.

The steps in his repudiation are fairly clear. Man and his reason are presumptuous. He is really no wiser than the animals, nor abler in the pursuit of knowledge, happiness, or goodness. Simplicity and trusting acceptance of life as it comes, such as we find in Socrates and Pyrrho, is both happier and better than self-conscious, learned premeditation. Even the philosophers admit this, though they do not mean to.

If the philosophers had found truth, they would have a right to their dogmatic pride; but they have not. All the proud presumption that they preach and practice is a barrier to Christian faith. When they try to define and thus limit God by their human reason and analogies, they are blasphemously impudent. Pyrrhonism is the best philosophical position both in itself and as a basis for Christianity.

Rational dogmatism, stoical humanism—call it what you will—is all wrong. Without God's grace man knows nothing and can know nothing. Stability is beyond his reach, and with it perfect knowledge, which is stable and eternal. The very mechanism of our cognition makes any certain knowledge of externals impossible. What can we do as creatures of flux? One thing only: learn its lesson and our own, know ourselves for what we are.

Montaigne's later additions to his conclusion sharpen it slightly but do not change its meaning. About Seneca's hope of rising above humanity he later comments: "That is a good saying and a useful desire, but equally absurd." For man is not equipped to do this for himself; God alone can do it for him. "It is for our Christian faith, not for his stoical virtue, to aspire to this divine and miraculous metamorphosis."

Montaigne's repudiation is complete. Stoical humanism does not lead to happy living. It cannot lead to our rising above humanity. Ethically as well as intellectually, for man in general as well as for Montaigne personally, it is the wrong road.

◆§ 4 §◆

Self-Discovery and Liberation
1577-1578

FOR the new war that arose from resentment against the pro-Protestant Peace of Monsieur (1576) neither side was especially well prepared. The king lacked the means for it, while the Huguenots were weakened by a general weariness of fighting and by the defection of several noble malcontents including the king's brother, formerly duke of Alençon and now of Anjou. It was on the king that fortune smiled this time; almost everywhere his forces triumphed. On September 17, 1577, at Bergerac, a treaty of peace was signed which again greatly reduced Protestant liberties. Since Henry III had won with little help from the League, he felt strong enough to write into the treaty a clause abolishing all leagues whatever. Though Protestant bands continued to ravage the south and deadly quarrels arose at court between Guise's faction and the favorites (*mignons*) of the king, a period of uneasy peace ensued.

It was indeed uneasy in and around Bordeaux. The city as a whole remained strongly loyalist, but powerful elements on either extreme, League and Protestant, were a constant threat to security. Twice Condé attempted vainly to take over the city for the Reformists. The mayor was the king's lieutenant general in Guyenne, Marshal de Biron, a loyal man and firm, but not tactful. All three qualities were needed, and were soon to be sought and found in Montaigne.

Of Montaigne's personal life during these two years little is known. A fifth daughter was born and died. He seems to have traveled a good deal, but we have no details. One important honor came to him without notice, the first of many from Henry of Navarre: the title of gentleman of his chamber (November 30, 1577). Now he held this position with two rival kings, Protestant Navarre as well as Catholic France. Thus his moderation as well as his loyalty had been formally recognized.

Few essays can be assigned securely to this period. Probably Montaigne was still working mostly on his longest chapter and reflecting on some of the consequences of Pyrrhonism and of his own abandonment of stoical humanism. For a while he may even have felt that he had little left to say. But "Que sçay-je?" is not a denial; it is a question. If it rejects one method of inquiry as useless, it suggests another.

Montaigne's skepticism is obviously limited; but whether mainly in time or in degree, it is hard to say. His alternation within the "Apology" between warmth and coolness toward Pyrrhonism may come from either change of attitude or inconsistency of statement. It is hard to say which, because we do not know just when and how this chapter was composed.

There is general agreement in dating the center of it, and what Villey calls Montaigne's "skeptical crisis," at around 1576. Strong evidence, external and internal, suggests that the framework which transformed Montaigne's critique of human reason into an "Apology for Raymond Sebond" was superimposed around 1579. But the rest of the chapter is hard to date. Villey suspects that it was composed in different strata. Zeitlin develops a good theory along the same lines: that the part on man and the animals was written around 1573–75; the Pyrrhonistic center around 1576; the framework and certain criticisms of Pyrrhonism, between 1578 and 1580. In short, he explains Montaigne's inconsistencies of tone and statement as changes of opinion and attitude.

They may be mainly a result of Montaigne's alternate playfulness and seriousness, which may be seen even within each of the layers that Zeitlin suggests. In polemic especially, Montaigne's love of irony and paradox often makes him reverse himself quickly. Even when he is praising Pyrrhonism and adopting its method, he virtually acknowledges that it is merely an intellectual game like the rest. And his treatment of conduct and attitude, whose importance our last chapter stressed, is quite consistent. All this suggests that except for the framework, the "Apology" may well be the work of two or three years, presumably 1575–77.

Whatever the precise solution to this problem, it is a limited skepticism that emerges from the "Apology." In Montaigne's eyes, Pyrrhonism is after all merely the best of a bad lot of systems; more a method than a creed; a means of beating down man's presumption; a fencer's trick to preserve faith by disarming reason on both sides. To use experience against reason as Montaigne does is the opposite of Pyrrhonizing, and he virtually admits it. The philosophers who have ruined common sense are fair game for the Pyrrhonist treatment; but the rest of us are still entitled to use common sense, and Montaigne does. He gives his hand away completely when in the heart of his Pyrrhonist demonstration he says that there are no first principles unless God has revealed them: "For every human presupposition and every enunciation has as much authority as another if reason does not make a distinction between them." This means that reason is helpless—except where it helps; that Montaigne is a Pyrrhonist—except where he is not.

Montaigne's skepticism is as finite in extent as in degree. His statements of his purpose make this clear. Man's false opinion of knowledge and its value, and the vanity and presumption that this breeds in him—these and these alone are the targets. When he hits others it is less from malice than from inattention arising from excitement in the sport. It is mainly in their peripheral extravagances that Montaigne attacks human reason and knowledge. What he mocks is our claims that we know what we cannot know. Never does he suggest that we can know too much or think too much about ourselves and our behavior.

He rarely criticizes experience. Since it deals simply and concretely with what happens and not with why it happens, he finds it far less suspect than reason. Where reason differs, he prefers to follow facts and results. He seems to disparage even Pyrrhonism when he calls it a way of using reason to cast doubt on the findings of experience. Many of his arguments for our intellectual helplessness—the illusions of the senses and the fact of flux—he derives as much from experience as from Pyrrho or Plutarch.

Although the "Apology" shows our incapacity for perfect knowledge, it does not consistently deny the value of the imperfect knowledge that we can have. Even without God's help, apparently, we must learn some wisdom from our variations, our errors, our follies. Obviously if we must, we can. If our knowledge cannot be perfect, it can still be useful. And that is what matters to Montaigne.

The "Apology" is Montaigne's declaration of complete intellectual independence. The stoical humanists that are his favorite targets were once his heroes and in some measure his teachers. Now he finds such serious flaws in them that they are heroes for him no longer. Now he frees himself wholly from their tutelage and looks within himself for instruction.

At the same time, to a certain extent at least, he is freeing himself also from Christianity as a way to goodness. He never quite admits this, but he seems to know it. Though his faith is sincere, his position is so extreme that this is logical. His God is so remote that man can do nothing to rise toward him either morally or intellectually; nor does his God apparently raise many men by the special action of his grace. The appalling practices of Montaigne's time seem to convince him that Christianity has hardly any moral effect at all. What goes under that name is a pretext for the worst treachery and cruelty. Since religion apparently does no more than philosophy to make man better, let him look within himself for a human code that will work.

THE GREAT RESOURCE

Montaigne's dilemma, when he saw the vanity of human knowledge, was not unlike that of Bacon, Descartes, and Pascal; but they had his conclusions to start with, and they were harder to satisfy. Whereas they wanted perfect truth, he was content with self-knowledge and happiness. His purpose from the very first was to enjoy life, and as soon as he was convinced that humanistic rationalism would not serve his purpose, he abandoned it for another method, a great new resource—self-study.

Self-study was no new idea in Montaigne's time. The maxim, "Know thyself," had been on the temple of Apollo at Delphi and on the lips of Socrates. Even Calvin had used it in his *Institutes*. It may have struck Montaigne first in the early pages of the book he translated, Sebond's "Natural Theology":

> Since nothing created is closer to man than man himself, he will remain very assured and very enlightened about everything that is proved concerning him, by himself, by his nature, and by what he knows certainly. . . . That is why man and his nature must serve as means, argument, and testimony to prove everything about man, to prove all that concerns his salvation, his happiness, his unhappiness, his evil, and his good; otherwise he will never be sure enough of it. So let him begin to know himself and his nature, if he wants to verify anything about himself. But he is outside himself, at an extreme distance from himself, absent from his own house, which he has never seen, ignorant of his worth, trading himself for something null, for a short joy, for a slight pleasure, for sin. So, if he wants to know his former value, his nature, his pristine beauty, let him return to himself and come back home.

The importance of knowing oneself is suggested but not fully brought out in the early essays. Montaigne says that he retired in order to let his mind settle in itself. For independence of others he urges withdrawal into oneself after first making ready. The worst he sees in our learning is that it lacks knowledge of and for ourselves. He relies on his own self-knowledge when he takes himself as a prime example of human inconsistency. His clearest early foreshadowing of his plan is in "Practice" (1573–74), when he concludes his story of his nearest approach to death with this comment: "This account of so slight an event is rather empty, were it not for the instruction I have derived from it for myself; for in truth, to grow reconciled to death, I think there is nothing like getting close to it. Now, as Pliny says, each man is a very good education for himself, provided he has the capacity to watch himself closely. This is not my doctrine, this is my study; and it is not the lesson of others, it is mine."

We have seen self-study become a rather important theme in the "Apology." As Montaigne sees it, man wastes his time trying to define, and thus limit, God, when he should be learning his own limitations. The know-it-alls who criticize Sebond do not seem to know even the difficulty of knowing themselves. If man knew anything at all, it would be himself, for he is closest and easiest. The all-important lesson of our weakness is not easy to learn, but Montaigne has done so by studying himself: "I who watch myself more closely, who have my eyes incessantly fixed on myself, like one who has not much business elsewhere . . . hardly would I dare tell the vanity and weakness that I find in myself." He does not yet say, as he will later, that all who do as he does will learn the same lesson; but he seems to feel it. Self-observation is already his basis for many generalizations about human variability. It can teach us the uncertainty of the senses better than Pyrrho, for "each man can furnish himself with as many examples as he pleases."

Since the "Apology" aims primarily to humble reason and vanity, Montaigne dwells more there on our limitations than on our resources. However, the message is already clear that we must look within to find these and become wise. As he wrote later: "Since philosophy has not been able to find any road to tranquillity that was good for all in common, let each man look for it individually!"

It seems to have been mainly in the years 1577–78 that Montaigne took full possession of his key idea. When he rejected the tutelage of others around 1576, he turned to the study of self. Three years later he was to make self-study the subject of his book. Meanwhile it had become his occupation.

His method now embodies the lessons of the "Apology." Reasoning and logic have no place; the instrument is judgment, the material experience. What reveals man most truly is rarely his public behavior, often the trivial, always the typical and the everyday.

Judgment is the key faculty for Montaigne. Though he sometimes equates it with common sense, he generally recognizes this vast difference: that judgment can see its own weakness and thus raise man above himself. Usually it is identical with understanding (*entendement*). It means the same thing as reason in the sense of *right reason* but contrasts with reason's other sense, *wrong reasoning,* by being close to the facts, patient, always ready to learn, cautious in reaching conclusions. It can be trained, and this is the heart of education. In the study of oneself it learns most and grows strongest; thus it is interdependent with self-study. It has no necessary connection with knowledge but is by far the more important of the two. Its jurisdiction is unlimited. An intellectual faculty, it is a guide in morals as well, deciding not only what is true but what is good. It is the part of man that teaches him how to live.

The study that teaches man how to live is that of himself. That is why it is so absolutely essential. Montaigne is like Socrates, whom he quotes as considering all knowledge but that of moral living a waste of time. "I take no stock," he writes, "in goods that

I have not been able to employ in the service of my life. . . . I have put all my efforts into forming my life. That is my trade and my work."

Montaigne has noted in the "Apology" that the most attainable as well as the most important knowledge is that of self. He is weary of the pedants who "perch astride the epicycle of Mercury" and claim to decide what makes the Nile ebb and flow, when they do not even understand themselves. Though he is not yet sure that self-knowledge is knowledge of man, at least he knows that it is real knowledge of a man. The old methods are too general and theoretical to teach us anything at all about anyone in particular. The popular Renaissance view of man as the microcosm is as useless here as scholastic logic or—Montaigne will tell us presently—as Aristotle's observations. These theories do not apply to a creature as vain, diverse, and undulating as man. Montaigne has seen this from the first. "Each bit plays its own game. And there is as much difference between us and ourselves as between us and others. . . . That is why, to judge a man, we must follow his traces long and carefully." Furthermore, we must judge from within, "sound the inside, and see what springs set us in motion." Obviously there is no one whose traces we can follow longer and more carefully than our own, no one we can know so inwardly and so well: "There is no reliable witness except each man to himself."

That self-study, finally, is a school of judgment, Montaigne does not so much state as assume. In the following passage, the sequence of ideas seems to show how closely the two are connected in his mind:

> Now these opinions of mine are, I find, infinitely bold and constant in condemning my inadequacy. In truth, this, too, is a subject on which I exercise my judgment as much as on any other. The world always looks straight ahead; as for me, I turn my gaze inwards, I fix it there and keep it busy. . . . I continually observe myself, I take

stock of myself, I taste myself. Others always go elsewhere, if they stop to think of it; they always go forward; as for me, I roll about in myself. This capacity for sifting truth . . . I owe principally to myself.

Until his new resource has met the test of time and pain, Montaigne does not claim for it all that he will later. But already he finds it the surest road to man's most essential knowledge, and he senses that beyond that knowledge lie wisdom and happiness. It is at this stage that he decides to make it the subject of his book.

THE IDEA OF THE ESSAY

It was probably in 1577–78 that the title of his book first came to Montaigne. Though one description of his plan cannot be dated securely, all the rest are of 1578 or later. The term *essay,* now so familiar, was new with him and still full of its literal meaning. His essays, he says, are the trials, or tests, of his judgment and his natural faculties, by which he seeks to reveal these faculties and this judgment.

It is also around 1578 that he first speaks of himself as the subject of his book. This idea is closely related to that of the essay. It is not that Montaigne never writes about anything but himself, but rather that he now realizes that to write at all is to portray oneself and finds in himself the unity of his book. Whatever he writes about, he is always judging, and he knows that his action in so doing is part of his portrait. He shows us Montaigne self-judging and self-judged—not only his conclusions but also his essays in judgment. This seems to be what an essay means to him: not only a test but also a revelation.

Judgment is a tool to use on all subjects and comes in everywhere. Therefore, in the tests (*essais*) that I make of it here, I use every sort of occasion. If it is a subject I do not understand at all, even on that I essay my judgment, sounding the ford from a good distance; and then, finding it too deep for my height, I stick to the bank. And this acknowledgment that I cannot cross over is a token of its effect, indeed one of those it is most proud of. Sometimes in a vain and nonexistent subject I try to see if judgment will find the wherewithal to give it body, prop it up, and support it. Sometimes I lead it to a noble and well-worn subject in which it has nothing original to discover, the road being so opened up and beaten that it can walk only in others' footsteps. There judgment plays its part by choosing the way that seems best to it, and of a thousand paths it says that this one or that was the most wisely chosen.

For the rest, I let chance itself furnish me with subjects, since they are all equally good to me; and I do not undertake to develop them completely and to the bottom of the vat. Of a thousand aspects that they each have, I take the one I please. I am prone to grasp them from some unusual and fanciful angle. I would certainly pick out richer and fuller subjects if I had any other purpose set than the one I have. Every action is fit to make us known.

Montaigne's only account of how he arrived at his plan is too self-disparaging to be taken at face value, though it seems to support the other evidence of his timing and his reasons. "Madam," he writes, "unless strangeness saves me, and novelty . . . I shall never get out honorably from such an enterprise. . . . It was a melancholy mood, consequently very much opposed to my natural temperament, produced by the gloom of the solitude into which I had cast myself some years back, which first put into my head this daydream of trying to write. And then, finding myself entirely void and empty of any other matter, I presented myself to me as theme and as subject. A wild and unnatural plan."

His main task is to see himself and describe himself as accurately as he can. His ideas may not be true, but he must give a true picture of his ideas. What he is trying to make known is not things but himself; not the measure of things but the measure of his sight. He claims no certainty unless it is in making known what he thinks and the extent of his knowledge of his subject. Hence he speaks his mind fully even in matters beyond his competence. "For likewise these are my humors and opinions; I offer them as what I believe, not what is to be believed."

His order may not be the most logical, but it must represent the way his mind naturally moves: "I have no drill sergeant to line up my parts other than fortune. . . . I want people to see my natural and ordinary step, just as out of step as it is." His language, he says, is "dry and thorny, with free and uncontrolled turns of expression; and I like it that way." The style, in short, must be the man himself; and as the essay plan matures in Montaigne's mind, it becomes just that. Pascal was probably thinking of Montaigne when he wrote of the beauty of the natural style: "You were expecting to find an author, and you find a man."

In order to be truthful, the portrait must change: for the subject changes with the passing years. Montaigne wants to represent the course of his humors, showing each of his parts at its birth; he wishes he had begun earlier so that he could recognize the progress of his changes. If he is altered tomorrow by learning something new, this, too, he will reveal.

Good or bad, handsome or ugly, the portrait must be true. In every way, as faithfully as possible, it must be the likeness of Montaigne.

> Whatever these absurdities may be, I have no intention of concealing them, any more than I would a bald and graying portrait of myself, in which the painter had drawn not a perfect face, but mine. . . .
>
> Even if I had been able to adopt some other style than my own ordinary one, and some other better and more honorable form, I would not have done it. . . .
>
> I want to be seen here in my simple, natural, ordinary fashion, without study or artifice; for it is myself that I portray.

In the essays written just before the first publication of his book, Montaigne is usually very disparaging of his plan. There seems to be something close to stage fright in his fear that his potential public of 1580 might think that to talk so trivially about oneself was proof positive of presumption. He knows that to condemn self-analysis on this ground is to throw out the baby with the bath, that his judgment is strong enough to assess him honestly; and he defends his plan stoutly in "Presumption." But he usually seems to feel that in order to be accepted as truthful he must be less truthful than modest. Hence the abundance of such statements as this: "I see well enough how little all this matters and is worth. . . . I am not obliged *not* to say stupid things, provided that I recognize them as such."

Self-portrayal Montaigne may sometimes belittle, but self-study never. In the earliest essays he had seen its value; beginning with the "Apology" he preached it as a duty; now he made it his main occupation and theme. His study of the follies of philosophy gave him confidence that he could do no worse. Already he had suggested, and soon he was to express clearly, certain independent convictions on which he acted. He feels that our attitudes, our wisdom, our moral code, must be our own, rooted in our being, based on what we are. If they are not, they are nothing. Consistency, wisdom, and happiness are based on independence and naturalness. Self-study reveals not only our nature but also our natural resources. It is on these, not on those of stoical humanism, that Montaigne now relies.

THE HAPPY PARADOX

We have noted already at some length how much the "Apology" dwells on the alliance between ignorance and happiness. The futility of logic against the gout, the stone that premeditation puts in our soul before we have it in our kidneys, the wisdom of the simple man who suffers only when he suffers—these are merely a few of Montaigne's variations on a favorite theme. Apparently while composing the "Apology," he came to a conclusion momentous in the growth of his confidence: that the mechanism of our knowledge is a guarantee of happiness as well as of ignorance.

One of his main reasons for denying that we can have certain knowledge of externals is that the soul has no direct experience of them or contact with them. "Our conception," he writes, "is not itself applied to foreign objects but is conceived through the mediation of the senses; and the senses do not comprehend the foreign object but only their own impressions. And thus the conception and semblance we form is not of the object but only of the impression and effect made on the sense; which impression and the object are different things. Therefore whoever judges by appearances judges by something different from the object."

Lacking this contact, the soul is virtually impotent to see things as they are, virtually omnipotent to see them as it wills. This notion occurs over and over again in the "Apology," under the inspiration of Pyrrho, as a proof of our incapacity for perfect knowledge. But it had already come to Montaigne from Seneca as a possible argument for our capacity to be happy; and he was to return to it often with growing confidence as the strongest of proofs. He did not specifically equate the two aspects of the idea. But they are so close, and his expressions of them so nearly identical, that it is hard to believe that they were not connected in his mind.

It is in the early essay, "That the Taste of Good and Evil Depends in Large Part on the Opinion We Have of Them" (1572), that Montaigne, following Seneca, first puts a case for the capacity of the soul for happiness which comes from what may be called its *arbitrariness*—that is to say, its power to make what it chooses of the impressions brought to it by the senses. The diversity of human opinion, he says, proves that knowledge enters into us not on its own terms but on ours, or at best by a compromise. Things being, as it were, at the mercy of the soul, it is up to us to take them as we will and apply them to our advantage. But this advice, he finds, works only in theory. In practice it may help us against poverty and death, the menace and the effect of which are magnified by imagination. It is no help, however, against pain. Pain is a thing of which the senses themselves give us certain knowledge; all we can do is to "oppose it and tense ourselves against it." Our only resource is the stoical strength and tension of the soul, and it cannot accomplish very much.

This idea does not appear again until the "Apology"; but there its frequent repetition shows its importance in Montaigne's thought. In the part on man and the animals, he locates this arbitrariness of the soul mainly in the imagination when he writes: "The privilege in which our soul glories, of reducing to her condition all that she conceives, of stripping all that comes to her of its mortal and corporeal qualities, of constraining all the things that she considers worthy of her attention to . . . leave aside . . . all accidents of sense, in order to accommodate them to her immortal and spiritual condition . . . this same privilege, I say, seems very evidently to belong to the beasts."

In the last part of the essay, the arbitrariness of the soul is used as one of the main proofs that we can have no certain knowledge of externals. "That things," Montaigne writes, "do not lodge in us in their own form and essence, nor make their entry into us by their own power and authority, we see clearly enough. For otherwise we should all receive them in the same way: the taste of wine would be the same in the mouth of a sick man as in the mouth of a well man. . . . Thus external objects surrender to our mercy; they dwell in us as we please." For cognition is an active, not a passive process; we know things by our faculty of knowing and thus on our own terms, not "through the power and according to the law of their own essence."

The senses are unreliable agents, as anyone can tell: nothing comes to us except falsified and altered by them. And the soul in turn tricks the senses. When we are angry, in love, irritated, or afflicted, we do not see things as they are. "It seems as though the soul draws the operations of the senses inward and occupies them.

Thus both the inside and the outside of man are full of falsity, weakness, and lies."

The main responsibility for our ignorance still falls to the soul's arbitrary treatment of sense impressions: "Since our condition accommodates things to itself and transforms them according to itself, we no longer know what things are in reality."

Already present, however, is the other side of the picture—the chance for happiness that this phenomenon offers. Just before the last-quoted remark Montaigne had again raised the question whether men can make of external events whatever they choose, and this time in such a way as to suggest clearly that they can: "Moreover, since the accidents of illness, madness, or sleep make things appear to us otherwise than they appear to healthy people, wise men, and waking people; since this condition has the power to give things another essence than the one they have . . . is it not likely that our normal state and our natural disposition can also assign to things an essence corresponding to our condition and accommodate them to us, as our disordered states do? And that our health is as capable of giving them some appearance as sickness?"

Montaigne's belief that the soul is arbitrary and irresponsible appears in several different forms in the essays of 1576–80. He finds our taste as unreliable as our knowledge, since things come into us not in their natural simplicity and purity but altered. He shows what power he now attributes to the soul when, in the essay on "Presumption," he exhorts it to support the body like a good husband. When, as we shall see shortly, the dreaded illness of the kidney stone strikes him in 1578, he uses against it diversion, not pure resistance, and he discovers that he is as happy as ever in spite of the pain.

In the final additions to the essays we see Montaigne fully enjoying the benefits of the happy paradox that the source of our ignorance is the source of our happiness. The soul, he finds, has an absolute power to make what it wills of all things when they enter its domain, whatever their intrinsic qualities may be outside. It can use even dreams and error to make us content. All we need is to direct it properly, and we are absolute masters of our happiness: "Wherefore let us no longer make the external qualities of things our excuse; it is up to us to reckon them as we will. Our good and our ill depend on ourselves alone."

Perhaps as much as any other concept, this one underlies the abounding optimism of Montaigne's late years. Not the strength of soul to which the early essays aspire but the very arbitrariness that denies us perfect knowledge gives us control over our happiness. The source of our inevitable ignorance is the greatest guarantee of our contentment. This delightful discovery, clear in the late essays, seems to be in Montaigne's possession already in the "Apology for Raymond Sebond." If not already clear there, it is certainly suggested and fully prepared by the play of his mind upon the positive as well as the negative aspects of the idea.

Another pleasant paradox occurred to Montaigne at about the same time. His apprehension in the earliest essays had been based on the insecurity of our condition. But now he examined and questioned, apparently for the first time, Seneca's statement that we can enjoy nothing which we fear to lose. Now he finds that the opposite is far truer, and that obviously in sexual matters, less obviously but generally elsewhere, security breeds boredom and satiety. "Difficulty," he writes, "gives value to things. . . . To forbid us something is to make us want it; to give it up to us completely is to make us disdain it: lack and abundance fall into the same disadvantage. . . . Desire and enjoyment make us equally unhappy."

In the years following the "Apology," Montaigne was not yet as great an optimist as he was to be later. But much of what appears to be pessimism springs from the fact that up to then he had been studying mainly human faults and foibles; the dignity and worth of man and life he treated later. The "Apology" does not deny that man can make himself happier and better; it merely points out that he has not done as well as he likes to think and that he may be going about it in the wrong way. It states clearly that he can improve himself by judgment and self-study. And "The Education of Children," written but a few years later, shows how high a human level can be attained by training the judgment wisely.

During the work of the "Apology" and since, Montaigne has abandoned the ill-fitting, hand-me-down armor of stoical humanism and replaced it by new resources, new armor of his own. The new suit fits him better and makes him happier; but he cannot be secure in it until he has tested it and seen how it can take punishment. Intellectually, he has convinced himself that it can do well; but he knows that intellectually you can prove almost anything. There still remains the question whether it is adequate, a question that only the test of experience can answer. The test and the answer are shortly to come in the form of Montaigne's illness.

ORDEAL AND TRIUMPH

Seldom has genius been more wrongheaded that was Jules Michelet in a well-known judgment on Montaigne. Though he granted that Montaigne was an exquisite writer, he could not abide his atmosphere: "I find in him at each moment a certain nauseating taste, as of a sickroom where the stale air is impregnated with the sad perfumes of the pharmacy. All this is *natural,* no doubt; this sick man is *Nature's man,* yes, but in his infirmities. When I find myself shut up in this padded library, I need air."

It is true that Montaigne suffered greatly from illness in his last fourteen years. He had headaches, dyspepsia, tooth trouble, failing eyesight, the quinsy that actually killed him, and, worst of all, renal calculus, or stones in the kidneys. His *Travel Journal* shows the frequency of his attacks. Often every few days, once three times in two days, a stone would form in his kidney, block his urine, and give him intense pain in the passage until finally it was voided. Often there was great pain even without a stone. This was one of the most dreaded diseases of Montaigne's and earlier times, and properly so. Montaigne knew and quoted what Pliny had said: "There are only three kinds of illness to avoid which it has been customary to kill oneself: the fiercest of all is the stone in the kidney when the urine is blocked by it."

Actually, Montaigne's sickness was fully as important in his thought and attitude as Michelet suggests, but with the opposite effect. He never loved health more nor had a healthier outlook than from the time it first struck. Its first attacks were in many ways as much a pivotal point for him as the "Apology." He had dreaded the disease, until it came, as the worst thing life had to offer. When he found that with his new comfortable philosophy he could endure it and still be happy, he was freed from apprehension and able for the first time to enjoy life to the full.

Until he was around forty his health had been excellent. He wrote in 1572 that he had had little dealing with pain thus far. A year or two later, it was most of his life that he had spent "in perfect and entire health . . . blithe and ebullient." And this is confirmed by other remarks elsewhere.

But inexperience of illness made him dread it. "This state, full of verdor and gaiety," he writes, "made me find the consideration of maladies so horrible that when I came to experience them I found their pains mild and easy compared with my fear." To be shut up in a room had seemed to him intolerable. The time came, and it was not so bad: "The strength of my apprehension added almost half to the essence and truth of the thing." But the worst he had had to endure up to then was boredom and confinement; even his close approach to death had not been a test by pain. He knew that pain, unlike even death, could not fail to be hard to endure.

The stone was precisely the accident of age that he feared most. His father had lived to be sixty-six in splendid health; then the stone struck, and seven years later he died in terrible pain. Montaigne had inherited much from his father, and he knew he might inherit this, too. "The fear of this illness," he wrote later, "used to frighten me when I did not know it except by the cries of those who could not bear it." It had even led him in perfect health to consider suicide: "I had thought many times in my own mind that I was going forward too far, and that in going such a long road I would not fail to get involved at last in some unpleasant encounter. I felt and protested enough that it was time to leave, that I should cut off life in the quick and in the breast, following the rule of the surgeons when they have to cut off some limb. But those were vain propositions."

Then, in the spring or summer of 1578, came the first terrible attack of the stone. A year and a half later, after many more of these, he was ready to assess their effect on him in the final chapter of Book Two, "The Resemblance of Children to Fathers." His apprehensive thoughts of suicide earlier he now dismissed as idle fancies: "I was so far from being ready to do that then that in eighteen months or thereabouts that have passed since I have been in this charming state, I have already learned to adapt myself to it. I am already growing reconciled to this colicky life; I find in it food for consolation and hope. So bewitched are men by their wretched existence that there is no condition so harsh that they will not accept it to keep alive."

The fact that Montaigne makes fun of himself here is a sign that he is content. He does it again when he calls his freedom from sufferings of the soul "a stupid and insensible disposition"—adding that he considers it "one of the best parts of my natural condition." Real physical hurts he does indeed feel keenly; but bad as they are, they are not so bad as his fear of them had been: "Foreseeing them in other days with feeble delicate vision softened by the enjoyment of that long and happy health and repose that God lent me for the better part of my life, I had conceived them in my imagination so unendurable that in truth I had more fear of them than I have found harm in them. Wherefore I continue to confirm this belief, that most of the faculties of our soul trouble the tranquillity of our life more than they serve it."

For now he is at grips with what he considers the most sudden, painful, mortal, and hopeless of diseases; and he is doing very well indeed.

I have already experienced five or six very long and painful bouts of it. However, either I flatter myself or else there is even in this condition enough to support a man whose soul is unburdened of the fear of death and also unburdened of the threats, sentences, and consequences with which medicine gives us a headache. But the very impact of the pain has not such sharp and piercing bitterness that a well-poised man should therefore go mad or give up hope. I have at least this profit from the colic, that it will complete what I had still not been able to do to myself to reconcile and familiarize myself completely with death: for the more my illness oppresses and bothers me, the less will death be something for me to fear. I had already accomplished this: to hold to life only by life alone. My illness will undo even this bond; and God grant that in the end, if its sharpness comes to surpass my powers, it may not throw me back to the other extreme, which is no less a vice, of desiring and loving to die.

Now that his fear of pain and death is gone, now that he can endure and even enjoy the life of pain, he can at last attack the histrionics of stoical humanism with real authority. I have always thought, he says, that insistence on rigid composure was foolish: "Why does philosophy, which has regard only for real substance and actions, go playing around with these vain and external appearances, as if it were training men for acting in a comedy?" Its business is to govern our understanding and to keep the soul, even when the body is in the pangs of colic, aware of itself and on its accustomed track, fighting and enduring pain and excited by the struggle, not shamefully prostrated by it. It is cruelty to ask more. If the body is relieved by complaining, twisting, or crying out, let it do so: "We have enough labor with the pain without adding a new labor by our reason."

But Montaigne is not saying all this to excuse any such weakness of his own. To his delight he has found that he can take the pain like a sage—or better yet, like a man:

> I say this to excuse those whom we see ordinarily crying out and storming in the shocks of the pain of this sickness. For as for me, I have passed through it until now with a little better countenance. Not that I give myself trouble, however, to maintain this external decorum; for I take little account of such an advantage. In this respect I lend the pain as much as it likes. But either my pains are not so excessive, or I bring to them more firmness than most people. I complain, I am vexed when the sharp pains afflict me, but I do not come to the point of despair or frenzy.

Moreover, the painless intervals are clear and fine. Thanks to his rational preparation, he says, nothing affects his soul but the pain itself, when it is present. And his enjoyment of a life in which pain and health alternate may be the main source of the optimistic view he expresses later, that life is a harmony of good and bad elements which are both necessary to our happiness.

For although his initiation into illness has been very hard, the results are amazingly good. "I find myself in a considerably better condition of life than a thousand others, who have no fever nor illness but what they give themselves by the fault of their reasoning."

Now for the first time Montaigne appears entirely free from fear. He has trusted in nature to take care of him, and nature has treated him well. Never before has he shown such complete confidence, and never from now on will he lose it.

His illness even fits in well with the new plan of his book. It is an addition to his subject, and one in which his self-knowledge and his experimental method make him fully as able as the doctors. More and more his book and his life are going naturally hand in hand, which is just what he wants. Now that he has found his subject and his confidence in life, he is ready to develop and enlarge them.

His optimism stands out clearly in the chapter on "The Education of Children," which was written in this period. The tone throughout is happy and free, the style richly personal. He shows how good men can be trained by his own method, trying out, essaying, and thus strengthening the natural faculties and, above all, the judgment. He admits now that the philosophy he has attacked so often is not the real thing but a prevalent counterfeit. There is also a true philosophy, which is the road to wisdom and happiness. And the road is open to all.

> The soul in which Philosophy dwells should by its health make even the body healthy. It should make its contentment, tranquillity, and gladness shine out from within; should form in its own mold the outward demeanor, and consequently furnish it with graceful pride, an active and joyous bearing, and an equable and good-natured countenance. It is *Baroco* and *Baralipton* that make their disciples wretched and grimy, and not Philosophy; they know her only by hearsay. Why, her business is to calm the tempests of the soul and to teach hunger and fevers to laugh—not by some imaginary epicycles but by crude, workable, and palpable reasons. . . .
>
> It is Philosophy that teaches us to live.

Montaigne's main evolution is now complete. Except for one key idea, what remains is the expansion and development of the views that he has thus far worked out and tested. Gone is the trial by apprehension, and with it the uneasy attraction toward the alien philosophy of stoical humanism. Happy and confident in life, in his method, his subject, and his natural faculties, he is ready to write freely and originally, and above all to live with joyful security. Once philosophy had meant learning how to die. Now it means learning how to live.

⁂ 5 ⁂

The Free Man

1578-1580

NATURE VERSUS ART

AT the heart of Montaigne's method, his plan, and all his thinking now, is the urge to be natural and avoid artificiality. Mr. Hiram Haydn has well brought out the importance of this trend to set "nature" above "art" in European thought of the time, especially in primitivism and in the conflict between Epicureanism, which aims at pleasure as the highest good, and stoicism, which aims at virtue. And the greatest spokesman of "nature" that he finds is Montaigne.

Montaigne's notion of what is nature and what is art in man underwent little change. There seem to be two main tests: whatever is found in other living creatures is natural; whatever makes for our happiness is natural. In a sense, the two criteria are one, for all creatures naturally seek happiness. In man Montaigne generally regards as natural the body, the necessary appetites and emotions, common sense and judgment. Generally unnatural, and always subject to unnatural use, are such dubious prerogatives as imagination and unbridled reasoning and their offspring ambition, presumption, avarice, insatiability, worry, and apprehension. Man even at his best is ignorant and frail, full of natural inclinations that cannot always be forced by will and reason. Art refuses to recognize our human condition; nature, wisely, knows us for what we are and makes the most of it.

From the first, Montaigne's deepest criticism of stoical humanism was that it is antinatural. It orders us to conquer instincts that nature has given us and wrongly assumes that we always can. It sets man in a sense out of nature; but unless we have God's extraordinary grace, we are neither above nor below the rest and must be brought back and confined within the barriers of nature's polity. Our antinatural "art" has led us astray.

Now the critique of art and praise of nature increases and at the same time changes. It becomes more solid and less sweeping, more a reasoned and qualified conviction and less a paradoxical sally. Whereas in the "Apology" Montaigne had criticized man mainly in terms of the animals, now he speaks of this cock-and-bull theriophily with such detachment as to seem not to take it too seriously: "When I encounter, among the more moderate opinions, the arguments which try to show the close resemblance of ourselves to the animals, and how much they share our greatest privileges, and how plausibly we are likened to them, then indeed I cut down a lot of our presumption, and gladly cast off this vain and imaginary kingship that people give to us over the other creatures."

Now Montaigne's new-found confidence is beginning to extend from himself to man in general. Since originally at least man was natural, our best models are not the animals but natural men. And recent discoveries have made such men accessible.

The center of Montaigne's critique of art by nature at this time is the chapter "Of Cannibals" (I:31), where he describes a Brazilian tribe encountered in 1557 by Villegagnon and his expedition. In 1562 three of them came to Rouen. Montaigne had a long talk with one, and later he had for a long time as a servant a simple and reliable man who had spent ten or twelve years among them. Obviously they intrigued him, and it may possibly have been his account of them that led La Boétie to toy with the idea of fleeing the corrupt Old World for the New. But Montaigne does not speak of them much in the early essays; it is sixteen or seventeen years after he saw them that he turns from humbling man before the animals to showing the folly of human art and the nobility of human nature.

There is nothing savage or barbaric about these people, he tells us now, except to our biased eyes that can see no perfection in any government or religion except our own:

> They are wild, just as we call wild the fruits that nature has produced by herself and in her natural course; whereas really it is those that we have changed artificially and led astray from the common order that we should rather call wild. In the former the genuine, most useful, and natural virtues and properties are alive and vigorous, which we have debased in the latter, and have only adapted them to the pleasure of our corrupted taste. . . . It is not reasonable that art should win the place of honor over our great and powerful mother nature. We have so overloaded the beauty and richness of her works by our inventions that we have quite smothered her. Yet wherever she shines forth in her purity, she wonderfully puts to shame our vain and frivolous attempts. . . . All our efforts cannot even succeed in reproducing the nest of the tiniest little bird, its contexture, its beauty and convenience; nor even the web of the puny and vile spider. . . .
>
> These nations, then, seem to me barbarous in this sense, that they have been fashioned very little by the human mind, and are still very close to their original naturalness. The laws of nature still rule them, very little corrupted by ours.

The result is a naturalness that Plato and Lycurgus should have known, a simple innocence that Montaigne describes in terms to be echoed by Shakespeare in *The Tempest:* "This is a nation . . . in which there is no sort of traffic, no knowledge of letters, no science of numbers, no name for a magistrate or for political superiority, no touch of servitude, riches, or poverty, no contracts, no successions, no partitions, no occupations but leisure ones, no care for any but common kinship, no clothes, no agriculture, no metal, no use of wine or wheat. The very words that signify lying, treachery, dissimulation, avarice, envy, belittling, pardon, unheard of."

We are pleased to call them barbarous, Montaigne goes on, and by the rules of reason they are. But we are infinitely worse. Our judicial torture, practiced in the name of piety and religion, is far more savage than their cannibalism. Indeed, we surpass them in every kind of barbarity.

True children of nature, they gratefully accept her bounty and are content to satisfy their needs. Indeed, the very wisdom of happiness is in them. Later Montaigne was to state his final ideal in the following terms: "It is an absolute perfection and virtually divine to know how to enjoy our being lawfully." Here already he credits his cannibals with this perfection when he says that at home they lack nothing, not even "that great thing, knowing how to enjoy their condition happily and be content with it."

It is not mere instinct or custom that gives them these qualities, Montaigne finds; it is reasoning and judgment. This is shown by the natural art of one of their songs, and even better by the things that amazed them most in France: a child ruling grown men, and some men starving while others gorged. "All this," Montaigne concludes ironically, "is not too bad. But wait! They don't wear breeches."

Montaigne even makes the untrousered cannibals the symbol of the candor he seeks in his book when he tells the reader at the outset that he wishes he could go them one better: "If I had belonged to one of those nations which are said to live still in the sweet freedom of nature's first laws, I assure you I should most gladly have portrayed myself here entire and wholly naked." For him, their nature is far better than our art.

NATURE, ART, HUMANNESS

But if nature is a better guide than art, still she must not be a tyrant. Now that Montaigne has shown the frailty of reason, he is ready to show its strength. It is in fact, in its best sense, the thing that sets man clearly above the rest of nature. "Since it has pleased God," he writes, "to present us with some capacity for reason, so that we should not be, like the animals, servilely subjected to the common laws but should apply ourselves to them by judgment and voluntary liberty, we must indeed yield a bit to the simple authority of nature, but not let ourselves be carried away by her tyrannically: reason alone must have the guidance of our inclinations."

This fact is most important, for in it lie the seeds of progress—if not for humanity, at least for the individual. It means that although we have not improved on nature—on the contrary—still we can. It means that the central antithesis in Montaigne's mind is no longer simply nature *versus* art but rather human nature *versus* misguided human art.

In effect, we now have three levels of human attitude and conduct: natural simplicity, humanistic art or artificiality, and a higher human naturalness that is beyond art. Montaigne speaks of these as progressive levels through which men may move from the third (in order of excellence) to the first. But what strikes him most is that extremes tend to meet. The third level is more like the first than is the second, and it is also perhaps the best way to reach the first. Montaigne's concept is precisely the one that Pope expresses in his couplet on the dangers of a little learning.

In the early essays and in the "Apology," Montaigne is mainly concerned, as we have seen, with the second and third levels of art and nature; but often we have glimpsed all three. Humble people are as brave as philosophers, the ignorant as wise as the learned. The simple take heaven by storm; the ordinary dogmatic learned are headed for hell; the Pyrrhonists, who have drunk deep enough to know their ignorance, are on the first level and ready, if God chooses, to be raised above all human levels.

In a chapter that is hard to date, "Vain Subtleties" (I:54), Montaigne tells of playing at home the game of finding extremes that meet. For example, *Sire* is used for kings and humble merchants, *Dame* for women of high quality or none. Democritus, he says, attributes to gods and animals keener senses than to men. Sexual impotence can arise from frigidity or overeagerness. Childhood meets second childhood in weakness of intellect. The *Essays* may fail to please simple or excellent minds but still find a public in between. Later Montaigne added many other excellent examples: abecedarian and doctoral ignorance, simple and profound Christians, good peasants and good philosophers, natural and perfect poetry. Already in the original version one case illustrates his general concept:

> Stupidity and wisdom meet at the same point of feeling and resoluteness in suffering human accidents. The sages master and command misfortune, the others ignore it. The latter are so to speak short of the accidents, the former beyond them. The sages . . . leap above them by the strength of a vigorous courage: they disdain them and tread them underfoot, having a strong and solid soul against which the arrows of fortune, when they come to strike, are forced to bounce off and be blunted. . . . Between these two extremes dwells the ordinary and middle condition of men: those who perceive ills, feel them, and cannot endure them.

These sages sound rather like those of the early essays, when Cato the Younger was Montaigne's favorite model. Now, together with a better method, Montaigne has found a better model, Socrates.

Curiously, Socrates is not listed among Montaigne's three most excellent men in the chapter of that name (II:36), which was probably written at about this time. But Cato is entirely absent from the essay; and we are led to interpret *excellent* as *preeminent* when we find that Montaigne's highest praise of his greatest man, Epaminondas, is that even in private life he was as good as Socrates.

Montaigne's new view of the three levels, with Socrates at the top, now appears in "Cruelty" (II:11). As in his earlier chapter on suicide, "Custom of the Island of Cea" (II:3), he offers here a sort of dialogue with himself in which the order of ideas appears to be that of his own thinking since he retired. Virtue, he begins, must be something nobler than an inborn inclination to goodness. It is a greater thing to master wrath by reason than not to feel it at all: "The one action might be called goodness; the other, virtue: for it seems that virtue presupposes difficulty, combat, and contrast, and that it cannot exist without opposition." Hence we call God good, but not virtuous. And therefore the stoics, Epicureans, and others have sought out pain and trouble, to test and strengthen their virtue. "Virtue refuses facility as a companion. . . . It demands a rough and thorny road; it wants to have either external difficulties to wrestle with . . . or internal difficulties raised for it by the disordered appetites . . . of our condition."

So far so good. But now Montaigne completely reverses himself: "I have come thus far quite comfortably. But after all this argument, it occurs to me that the soul of Socrates, which is the most perfect that has come to my knowledge, would be by my account a soul with little to recommend it: for in that person I cannot conceive of any effort of vicious desire." Socrates' reason is too strong to allow any bad impulse even to arise. Are we to say then that he is not virtuous, that virtue is dependent on vice and weakness? What of the virtue that actually enjoys pain? The younger Cato must have enjoyed his suicide as a trained athlete enjoys a good test of his strength. Both men are above painful and struggling virtue; and Socrates is the highest of all, taking death with even less strain than Cato, gaily, simply, in his stride. "Cato will please pardon me; his death is more tragic and tense, but the other is still, I know not how, more beautiful."

Both men have trained their fine natures by practicing the precepts of philosophy. No place is left for vice in either one. Virtue has become a habit, part of their temperament, "the very essence of their soul . . . its natural and ordinary gait." Obviously this is perfection, superior to ordinary virtue even as that is superior to innocence.

In some ways this system of levels is not as tidy as it seems. God's presence on the "lowest" plane is striking, and at least suggests that virtue, or moral strength, may be on a lower plane than goodness. Furthermore, Montaigne does not really seem to know where to place himself. Naturally he says that he belongs at the bottom. His is a virtue, he says, or rather innocence, that is accidental and fortuitous; he was luckily born good-natured and hating most vices but has shown little strength in resisting passions; he does not know how to foster quarrels and conflict within him. However, he seems to contradict himself. His excesses have not been remarkable, he says, and have never corrupted his judgment. He has not opposed his vices enough, "except to control them and keep them from mixing with other vices; for they mostly hold and are intertwined together, if you don't watch out. Mine I have kept apart and confined, as isolated and as simple as I could."

In short, his is no mere passive innocence. If he belongs in the lowest class, he is not so far from the others as he claims. Already he appears to suspect that the middle level of struggle may be a detour on the road from innocence to virtue. Though his position still seems a little confusing, several things are clear. Cato is high, but Socrates is higher. Cato, the athlete of virtue, still resembles the others on the middle level; his death is tense and tragic. Socrates seems immune to tragedy and tension. Though the innocence of nature unadorned is placed below the virtue of human art, still the highest virtue is beyond art, compounded of nature and habit. And habit is not a form of art; soon Montaigne will call it a second nature.

In this chapter, however, it is clearer than ever that Montaigne's ideal is no longer just nature, but human nature. Just as he now writes elsewhere that man must not be nature's slave, and that La Boétie added to rich inborn gifts by study, so here Socrates and Cato have improved their good natures by practicing the rules of philosophy. As we shall see shortly, Montaigne's confidence in man's possibilities at this time is shown best in his chapter on education. For an intransigent champion of nature against art like Rousseau, education must be largely negative, to keep the child uncorrupted by art. For Montaigne, education can be positive. Hard as it is to force our inclinations, we can train them by habit and control them by judgment. More and more judgment is the key faculty for Montaigne, the one by which man can and should rise above mere nature.

HUMAN NATURE

"Of all the opinions antiquity has held of man, the ones I embrace most willingly and adhere to most firmly are those that despise, humiliate, and nullify us most. . . . It seems to me that the nursing mother of our falsest opinions, public and private, is the over-good opinion that we have of ourselves."

This is still the burden of a great many of Montaigne's remarks in 1578–80, as it was in the early essays. He is no misanthrope, but contempt for human presumption often makes him sound like one. His attacks on man have really been aimed at man's self-conceit, at the common humanistic view of man as lord of creation, capable of everything, constant and consistent, ruled by will and reason. Now that he has spoken his mind on the subject in the "Apology," Montaigne is more ready to point out man's possibilities as well as his limitations. But when he generalizes about man, he is usually cautious in expressing his new confidence.

By now he has treated quite fully a wide variety of human limitations. In rather random order, these include the power over us of fear, imagination, custom, natural inclinations, impulsion from without and within, wine, illness, conscience, the stars, insects, sense impressions, fortune, and heaven knows what else; our impotence for knowledge, goodness, and happiness; our inelasticity not only in achievement but even in aspiration. But now as never so fully before he begins to see the qualities of our defects.

The facts of human nature that seem to strike him most now are these: Man is a child of nature, a prodigal son who has strayed but belongs at home. He is made up of soul and body, though he is prone to forget it. He varies and changes so much that in a way he can hardly be said to exist. But stoical humanism is no longer the cure for man's variability, since it is necessarily inconsistent. Change is a part of man's natural condition. He may limit it by his awareness of it, but some of it he must simply accept. From what he is he can learn what he can be. By consenting —and learning—to be himself, he can be somebody. If he recognizes and accepts his limitations, his possibilities are great.

For one thing, some of our weaknesses contradict each other or play into the hands of our strengths. Diversion, which Montaigne has not yet discussed but has practiced, is a benefit of our inconstancy. Our inability to force our natural inclinations is a source of consistency that can even be good; for many fine natures maintain themselves despite a bad education. Custom and habit, those dangerous tyrants, can be beneficent; they can train us, as Montaigne points out, to use our feet for hands and to carry a calf until it is an ox; they can conquer the fear of death, as philosophy cannot, and lead to the highest type of virtue. The variety of human judgments in time and place, and the variability of our own, are reasons for skepticism and humility; but our awareness of this is wisdom, for wisdom is the knowledge of ourselves and of our place in the scheme of things.

Particularly in the realm of enjoyment our resources are many. Our vulnerability is a condition of satisfaction. The conscience that punishes can also grant the most gratifying of rewards. Ignorance goes hand in hand with happiness as with virtue: the cannibals who trust purely in nature live happily and nobly in her loving care. Best of all, the soul's arbitrary treatment of sense impressions guarantees that we can be as happy as we will. In the earliest essays it was the soul, except in a few sages, that needed the body's help. Now the arbitrary soul can and must govern and aid the body:

The body has a very great part in our being, it holds a high rank in it; so its structure and composition are well worth consideration. Those who want to split up our two principal parts and sequester them from each other are wrong. On the contrary, we must join and attach them together again. We must order the soul not to draw aside and entertain itself alone, scorning and abandoning the body (nor can it do so except by some hypocritical monkey trick), but to rally to the body, embrace it, cherish it, assist it, control it, advise it, set it right and bring it back when it goes astray; in short, marry it and be a real husband to it, so that together they may produce results not different and contrary but harmonious and uniform.

Even the difficulty of knowing others has its good side. For we can know ourselves as no other can know us; we can be our own best judges, perhaps our only judges. This is one of our greatest freedoms. Without self-knowledge we are constantly anxious about other people's opinions of us. In one of the earliest essays Montaigne had listed contempt as a thing to fear; now he no longer does. For if we know ourselves, we can replace anxiety with the security of independence. Judgment and conscience, armed with self-knowledge, will make not cowards of us all, but free men.

The clearest sign of Montaigne's faith in the possibilities of human nature is his faith in good education. Where early he had been negatively critical ("Pedantry," I: 25), now in "The Education of Children" (I: 26) he is mainly constructive. The whole chapter shows what can be done by proper training. The wise tutor, who watches and listens as well as talks, will develop our natural faculties. He will train us through habit to gain toughness of body, modesty and readiness to learn, and the freedom of versatile adaptability. History will give us experience and perspective in time; travel, in space. Both will help to form our judgment, which is the main aim of education. So will concentration on meaning and substance instead of memorization; and so, above all, will constant practice. Taking nothing on authority but judging everything by ourselves, we can truly fashion our soul to love virtue and to hate vice for their own sakes, not from impotence or for fear of punishment.

Thus education appears to Montaigne as difficult but vitally important. The judgment that it fashions is the key to independent moral stature and moral living. It can train apparently all but a few men to be free, judicious, versatile, wise, and happy.

Montaigne's awareness of all these possibilities gives him much to look forward to and live for even in the grip of painful illness. Free from worry and from compulsion to be something other than he is, secure in the knowledge, gained by self-study, of what he may properly expect of himself and what he may not, he can now make the most of life. The power of the soul over sense impressions helps him in pain; freedom from apprehension gives him full enjoyment of health. Even the alternation of pain and well-being, typical of life in general, adds zest to the intervals of health.

I welcome health with open arms, full, free, and entire, and whet my appetite to enjoy it, the more so as it is rarer and less ordinary with me. So far am I from troubling its repose and sweetness with the bitterness of a new and constrained way of life. The animals show us well enough how many maladies and how much weakness the agitation of our mind brings us. . . .

I am at grips with the worst of all illnesses, the most sudden, the most painful, the most fatal, and the most irremediable. . . . However, up to this moment I maintain my spirit in such a state that, provided I can bring constancy to it, I find myself in a considerably better condition of life than a thousand others, who have no fever nor illness but what they give themselves by the fault of their reasoning.

Finally, Montaigne finds the enjoyment of life, for which the free man who knows himself is so admirably fitted, perfectly proper and legitimate. Nobler beings, he says, have the right to scorn our being, but not we ourselves; to do so is a malady peculiar to man. It is equally vain to try to be other than we are. If we accept ourselves as we are and life as it is, we have much to enjoy.

HUMAN DIVERSITY

By the year 1580, when he publishes the first version of the *Essays,* Montaigne has either stated or suggested all his final key ideas but one—that of human solidarity and unity. He is still strongly individualistic in two ways: in his predominant concern with himself and in his feeling of the tremendous differences between men.

He is beginning to be a little less so. More and more often he generalizes about man, especially about his limitations and possibilities. He sees clearly the fundamental unity of kings and peasants, cannibals and Europeans. Even the elements of his final plan to study man through himself are now present, though not put together, in "Presumption" (II:17). For here Montaigne calls man, as well as himself, the subject of his study; and he portrays himself as a thoroughly average specimen (thus a characteristic subject) whose judgment (which can make him a trustworthy reporter) is his only distinctive quality. He is always greatly concerned with sociability and communication. Sympathy and insight have made him a cosmopolite in time and space. He has found friends and brothers of the most varied sorts: La Boétie, Cato, Socrates, Plutarch, the ignorant, cannibals, even animals.

However, he is not yet ready to admit that man cannot live

fully for himself unless he lives somewhat for others. He has not yet added any corrective to his self-centered statement in "Solitude": "The greatest thing in the world is to know how to belong to oneself."

And even his generalizations seem to escape him against his better judgment. He is still very wary of all broad statements. Later he will strike a balance; now it is diversity that he sees everywhere. With this theme the *Essays* of 1580 begin and end. In his very first chapter Montaigne defines man as a marvelously vain, diverse, and undulating object, on which it is difficult to found any constant and uniform judgment. He begins Book Two by stressing the inconsistency that makes us so different from ourselves, and ends it with the differences between us and others. Here are the very last words of the first edition of the *Essays:*

> I do not at all hate opinions contrary to mine. I am so far from being vexed to see the discord between my judgments and others', and from making myself incompatible with the society of men because they are of a different opinion than mine, that on the contrary, since variety is the most general form that nature has followed, I find it much more novel and rare to see our humors and opinions agree. And perhaps there were never in the world two opinions entirely and exactly alike, any more than two faces. Their most intrinsic quality is diversity and discord.

Though this diversity does not disturb Montaigne, it is what strikes him most in mankind. He still feels himself simply an individual, not a member of a homogeneous group; his portrait is still that of an individual and little more. One essential element of his final thought is yet to come.

6

The Discovery of Others

1580-1586

MONTAIGNE'S life during these years was busy, varied, useful, and thoroughly involved with others. His main concern had long been with himself alone; now he extended it. His hail and farewell to the reader in 1580 shows how much confidence he had gained by then, but also how much he still lacked: "Thus, reader, I am myself the matter of my book; you would be unreasonable to spend your leisure on so frivolous and vain a subject. So farewell from Montaigne, this first day of March, 1580." There is a "take-it-or-leave-it" touchiness in these and other contemporary remarks about his book that is a far cry from the friendly confidence of the final essays. Only once had Montaigne felt himself fully understood, and that was by a friend, now seventeen years dead, who had been a good and remarkable man. Experience of the evil times suggested that he would not see the like of him again. As he cast his bottle into the sea, he seemed to feel little assurance that any finder would understand his message. A few had seen certain essays in manuscript and had liked them; but they were friends. At times Montaigne seemed to wonder quite seriously whether he was a mere eccentric with delusions of grandeur about his "wild and unnatural plan." His conviction that all men are very different was an insuperable obstacle to complete confidence. He still needed a sense of human unity and solidarity.

He gained it mainly from four experiences: his trip through Germany, Switzerland, and Italy; the success of his *Essays;* his two terms as mayor of Bordeaux; and his wanderings with his family during the plague.

THE TRIP

In the spring of 1580 the first edition of the *Essays* (Books One and Two) was published by Simon Millanges in Bordeaux. Montaigne came to court for a while, presented Henry III with a copy, and served in his king's army at the siege of La Fère. When his friend Philibert de Gramont (husband of "the great Corisande") was killed there, he accompanied the body to Soissons. Soon afterward he set out on a seventeen-month tour of the sights and mineral baths of Germany, Switzerland, and Italy. Actually he did little more than pass through the first two countries to spend over a year in Italy, mainly in Rome and at the baths of La Villa near Lucca but with many trips to Florence, Pisa, Lucca, Loreto, and elsewhere. With him were his youngest brother Bertrand, sieur de Mattecolom, a brother-in-law, and two other gentlemen, besides a secretary and many servants.

It has been conjectured that this was in part a diplomatic mission, and argued rather strongly that Montaigne was acquainting himself with Italy in the expectation of being named ambassador to Venice. Other motives for the trip are certain. Montaigne's curiosity was enormous. His eagerness to see his cultural homeland, Rome, was very strong, though according to his secretary "he desired less to see it than the other places, since it was known to every man. . . ." Montaigne was ill, and mineral baths offered a natural and harmless way to seek the priceless boon of health.

More important, perhaps, was the need of a vacation from home and from France. "There is scarcely less trouble," he had written, "in governing a family than an entire state. . . . Domestic occupations are no less importunate for being less important." Retirement had been far from solving all his probems. It wearied and bored him to manage his house, and he was ready for a vacation from his wife. The condition of France made him so heartsick that he shocked his prosaic secretary into reporting: "In truth he [Montaigne] mingled into his judgment a bit of the passion of scorn for his country, which he held in hatred and indignation for other considerations. . . ." As Montaigne himself writes later, "I know well what I am fleeing from but not what I am looking for. . . . It is always a gain to change a bad state for an uncertain one." He knew that his restlessness was vanity and folly, but he accepted this now as a part of being human.

A final motive was Montaigne's conviction, born of fruitful experience, that travel is one of the best forms of education. He recommends it strongly and repeatedly for his ideal pupil: "Mixing with men is wonderfully useful, and visiting foreign countries, not merely to bring back, in the manner of our French noblemen, knowledge of the measurements of the Santa Rotonda, or of the richness of Signora Livia's drawers, or, like some others, how much longer or wider Nero's face is in some old ruin there than on some similar medallion; but to bring back knowledge of the temperaments and ways of those nations, and to rub and polish our brains by contact with those of others."

This was the way Montaigne traveled—not as an ordinary sightseer or an antiquary but as a man seeking experience of others and their ways, wanting to meet them on their own terms and in their own language. Exposure to such variety, he felt, is a great source of perspective in judgment.

> Wonderful brilliance may be gained for human judgment by this contact with people. We are all huddled and concentrated in ourselves, and our vision is reduced to the length of our noses. Socrates was asked where he was from. He did not answer "Athens" but "the world." . . .
>
> This great world . . . is the mirror in which we must look at ourselves to recognize ourselves from the proper angle. All in all, I want

it to be the book of my student. So many humors, sects, judgments, opinions, laws, and customs teach us to judge sanely of our own, and teach our judgment to recognize its own imperfection and natural weakness; which is no small lesson. . . . The pride and arrogance of so many foreign pomps, the puffed-up majesty of so many courts and dignities, strengthens our sight and makes it steady enough to sustain the brilliance of our own without blinking. . . . And likewise for other things.

The record of Montaigne's trip is in a journal of about three hundred pages, partly dictated and partly written by himself, mostly in French but partly in Italian. Not intended for publication, it was first discovered and printed in 1774. Its greatest interest is in showing Montaigne in action when he does not expect his doings to be published, and thus making it possible to check on his candor in the *Essays*. It is also interesting on its own account, as a day-to-day record of a year and a half of his life.

The many details of meals and accommodations in the *Travel Journal* seem to many to give Montaigne away as a rather petty-minded sensualist. But he knew how every action reveals us, and how hard it is for a tourist to get beneath the skin of another country. Thus after a long stay he remarks ruefully that he would have liked Rome even better if he could have tasted it more privately; but for all his craft and effort, he has known it only by its public visage. Intimate knowledge being almost inaccessible, external observations must suffice. Wherever he went, his secretary tells us, he visited inns and boarding houses to try out all the commodities of the various cities. From all the details that he recorded in Basel about churches, houses, clocks, furniture, interiors, eating habits, scrubbed and polished woodwork and floors, ingeniously contrived spits, three- or four-hour meals at tables laden with food, there emerges a sketchy portrait of a conscientious, tidy, and comfort-loving people. And the proof that Montaigne found some such meaning in these details is in a curious remark about the Inn of the Rose at Innsbruck: "Around the beds there were curtains in some; and to show the humor of the nation, they were beautiful and rich, of a certain form of cloth, cut and open-worked, moreover short and narrow, in short no use for what we use them for." If bed curtains can show the humor of a nation, so can most of the other details of living habits that Montaigne relates.

One of the most striking things about the *Journal* is the picture of Montaigne living as far as he can the life of the people he sees—not merely buying a cane here or a straw hat there, but always adopting the customs of the places where he goes and even writing a good part of his journal in Italian.

Naturally it is the secretary who remarks on this most. After a month on the road he writes: "Monsieur de Montaigne, to try out completely the diversity of conduct and ways, everywhere let himself be served in the manner of each country, no matter what difficulty he encountered in so doing. In Switzerland, he says, he suffered none, except having at table only a little six-inch cloth for a napkin." A few days later at Lindau the same theme occurs: "at all events, he preferred the conveniences of that country to the French, beyond comparison, and conformed to them even to drinking wine without water." The first of several times that Montaigne leaves his escutcheon at a lodging he has liked, it is "on behalf of his hostess, according to the humor of the nation." In Augsburg comes a real disappointment. Montaigne has a cold, and holds his handkerchief to his nose in church, hoping still to be inconspicuous since he is unattended and simply dressed. But on better acquaintance, some townspeople tell him that this was remarked on; and the secretary concludes: "At last he fell into the vice that he most avoided, that of making himself noticeable by some mannerism at variance with the taste of those who saw him; for as far as in him lies, he conforms and falls into line with the ways of the place where he happens to be, and in Augsburg he wore a fur cap around the town."

Montaigne himself does not speak of this habit in the *Journal,* presumably because he finds it wholly natural; but his actions show his eagerness to experience other men's ways. He goes out of his way not only to discuss his and other religious faiths with experts but to observe all kinds of ceremonies at first hand: Calvinist, Zwinglian, and Jewish services, an exorcism, a circumcision, and a host of religious celebrations in Rome. Though he is far from neglecting the observances of his own cult, his consuming curiosity about other ways is shown by his secretary's report that in Mulhouse "Monsieur de Montaigne went to see the church; for they are not Catholics there." In Rome Montaigne makes himself an able guide to the city and puts great effort into securing the title of citizen of that most cosmopolitan town; at La Villa he gives dances and himself takes part as dancer and as judge. There, too, he decides to write his *Journal* in Italian, and continues until he crosses into France again. Even though he writes the language easily, he cannot express himself fully and personally; as a passage in the *Essays* later shows, it is still a diminution and a constraint to him to do so. In a man not prone to labor over learning or linguistics for their own sake, this effort shows a very strong concern with living the life of other countries as thoroughly as he can.

Montaigne's desire to try out other ways is born of sympathy and begets sympathy. He is irritated at the authors of the ridiculous reports he has read about the wildness and discomfort of the countries he visits. He finds much to enjoy and admire wherever he goes. "They are a very good nation," he writes of the Swiss, "especially to those who conform to them." The people around Plombières on the Franco-German border are also "a good nation," free, sensible, and law-abiding. From Bolzano he writes to François Hotman how much he has enjoyed his stay in Germany and in particular the courtesy, justice, and security he has found there. He finds the Roman upper classes as courteous and gracious as can be, despite their poor press among arrogant and parochial Frenchmen. He enjoys the air of Rome and all the pleasant diversions the city offers. Even what disappoints him at first he later comes to enjoy. On his third short visit to Florence he admits that it is rightly called "the beautiful"; a little later he acknowledges that he has nearly always been well lodged in Italy and that all he really lacks in Lucca is a good friend.

And the people that Montaigne likes like him. Whether or not the Pope raised his slipper slightly—as Montaigne likes to believe—when he went to kiss it, he certainly gave the Frenchman a friendly greeting and helped him get his Roman citizenship. Montaigne is readily admitted to the Vatican Library, though the French ambassador is not. He is very well treated, as we shall see shortly, by the papal censor. The distinguished Jesuit Maldonado seeks him out. One tribute to his judgment must have pleased him particularly. Much as he smiled at medicine, he had shown clearly what it needed to become a science. Now he finds himself called on more than once to decide between the grave sons of Aesculapius. "This same day," he writes at La Villa, "certain doctors, having to hold an important consultation for a young lord, Signor Paolo Cesi (nephew of Cardinal Cesi), who was at these baths, came to ask me at his behest to be good enough to hear their opinions and arguments, because he was resolved to rely wholly on my judgment. I laughed about it to myself. Other similar things happened to me often enough, both here and in Rome."

Perhaps the clearest sign of his popularity is his simple account of his return to the baths of La Villa: "There were great welcomes and warm greetings, which I received from everyone. In truth it seemed that I had come back home."

For in the month and a half he had spent earlier at La Villa, the man who feared that La Boétie had spoiled him for ordinary acquaintanceships had shown himself an excellent mixer. Besides making friends as he went along, he had given at least two parties. On Whitsunday (May 14, 1581), he writes that "I gave a peasant girls' dance after dinner, and I danced in it myself so as not to appear too reserved." A week later it was a really big dance with prizes open to the public. It was customary for wealthy visitors to give these, and Montaigne wanted to offer the first one of the year. He had it announced five or six days in advance, sent for prizes to Lucca (two prizes for men, nineteen for women), hired five fife-players for the day, and sent special invitations to the dance and supper after to all the noblemen and noblewomen at the baths. Over a hundred people came, besides the natives. When it came time to distribute the prizes, he cut his way deftly through ceremony to reach a happy arrangement with the noblest of the ladies:

> I told them that lacking the skill and boldness to judge such beauties and graces and nice manners that I saw in these girls, I begged them to assume this charge of judging and to distribute the prizes according to merit. We were held up on ceremony for a bit because they refused to assume this charge as though it was too much sheer courtesy. Finally I suggested this condition, that if they would be good enough to take me into their council, I would give my opinion. And this was the result, that I went picking out with my eyes now this one, now that; wherein I did not fail to have regard for beauty and grace, pointing out that the charm of the dance consisted not only in the movement of the feet, but in the carriage and grace and charm of the whole person. . . . One refused the prize. She sent to beg me that for her sake I should give it to another girl; which I did not consent to. The other was not one of the most attractive. . . . I would give the present that seemed right to me to the lady, kissing it; and she, taking it, would give it to the girl, saying graciously: "Here is this Lord Knight who is giving you this fine present: thank him."—"On the contrary, you are obliged to Her Ladyship, who picked you out from so many others as deserving a prize. I am very sorry that the present is not more worthy of such and such a quality of yours"—and I named these according to what they were. The same thing was done promptly with the men.

Montaigne found it a treat to see peasant girls who dressed and danced as well as any ladies. Candidly he says that he invited everyone to supper, "because the banquets in Italy are nothing but a very light meal by French standards. A few cuts of veal and a few pairs of chickens is all." He specifically invited to the table a peasant woman called Divizia, who could neither read nor write but was brought up on Ariosto and composed impromptu verse with wonderful facility, including this time some in Montaigne's honor. Altogether the guests and the host seem to have had a delightful time.

Some of Montaigne's gaiety, to be sure, springs from new places as well as new people. He compares travel to reading a good new book. He is eager for new impressions, having no plan but to wander in unknown places, capable of setting out for Cracow or Greece if he had only himself to consider. The valley of the Inn seems to him the most delightful landscape he has ever seen. Even extreme pain cannot spoil the scenery near Narni: "I had my colic very badly, which had gripped me for twenty-four hours and was then in its last fits; however, I did not fail to enjoy the beauty of that place." Altogether the secretary, who must have worked for him before, finds his master gayer than ever: "I never saw him less tired or complaining less of his pains; having his mind, both on the road and at the lodgings, so keyed up to what he encountered, and seeking out all occasions to talk to strangers, that I think this diverted his trouble."

There is no reason to doubt the secretary's word. Such courageous high spirits, which later inspired Sainte-Beuve to write the friendliest of his articles on Montaigne and conclude it by calling him "the wisest Frenchman that ever lived," are new. Here for the first time we see Montaigne fully practicing his final philosophy of serene acceptance. For days on end, sometimes for weeks, he endured the sharpest torment from the stone and other ailments. One of his worst attacks culminated on August 24, 1581.

For about ten days the stone, abetted by stomach trouble, toothaches, and headaches, had kept him in constant pain that mounted relentlessly to agony. At last he got rid of a big stone.

> Finally, on the morning of the 24th, I pushed down a stone that stopped in passage. I remained from that moment until dinner without urinating, though I wanted to very much. Then I got my stone out, not without pain and bleeding before and after the ejection. It was of the size and length of a little pine cone, but as thick as a bean on one end, and it had exactly the shape of the masculine member. It was a very happy thing for me to have been able to get it out. I have never ejected one comparable in thickness to this one; I had judged only too well by the quality of my urines what was to happen. I shall see what the sequels will be.
>
> There would be too much weakness and cowardice on my part if, sure of finding myself in a position to die in this manner, and moreover with death approaching every instant, I did not make every effort before coming to it to be able to endure it without trouble when the moment has come. For after all, reason recommends to us to receive joyously the good that it pleases God to send us. Now the only remedy, the only rule, and the unique knowledge, to avoid all the ills that besiege man from all sides and at every moment, whatever they be, is to make up our minds to suffer them humanly, or to end them courageously and promptly.

But even more than Montaigne's simple courage, his great sociability is new. From the earlier essays one would expect him to seek to learn from others, but not to like them so much. These are not sages—or cannibals—that he enjoys wherever he goes; nor are their customs dictated solely by reason or nature. Most of these people are the vulgar, and the customs are as irrational and arbitrary as any. Yet Montaigne enjoys them; and, worse yet, he seems to accept this deplorable fact with happy equanimity. As he meets people of many countries, ranks, and kinds, he makes friends with them and finds things in common; as he tries out other ways, he learns better than ever how superficially they differ from his own and how important are the underlying links. These are perhaps the most vital experiences of the trip in the development of his thought.

THE SUCCESS OF THE ESSAYS

Already we have noted Montaigne's fears before 1580 that his book would not find a public free enough from ceremony to take it on its merits and see the vast importance of this apparently trivial and presumptuous business of self-study. Generally he had taken pains to guard against a cool reception by claiming to write only for his friends.

The success of the *Essays* of 1580 pleased him and may have surprised him a little. "The favor of the public," he writes, "has given me a little more boldness than I had hoped. . . . Certainly I am grateful to nice people who deign to take my feeble efforts in good part." Later he will add that the wider his public, the more he is appreciated; in Gascony they think it comical to see him in print; he buys the printers in Guyenne, elsewhere they buy him.

Besides his own comments, there is evidence enough that the book was a success and that the author was pleased. Henry III must have seemed to like it, or Montaigne would not have replied to his compliments as he did: "Sire, then Your Majesty must necessarily like me, since my book is agreeable to you, for it contains nothing else but a discourse on my life and actions." This is the first commendation that we know of. Not so long after came the second, more weighty though not unmixed, from the papal censor.

What happened was this. When Montaigne first arrived in Rome, his books were taken from him at the customs to be examined, as was the practice. Surprised and disconcerted that he was in for a scrutiny so strict that certain German anti-Protestant books had been held suspect because they mentioned the errors they were combating, he still was relieved that he happened to have no condemned books on him. It was four months later that the *Essays* were returned, on the day after Palm Sunday of 1581. They had obviously been studied thoroughly; but the criticisms were mild, the fideism of the "Apology" was tacitly accepted, and the interview was a duel in politeness:

Today, in the evening, my *Essays* were returned to me, corrected according to the opinion of the learned monks. The *Maestro del Sacro Palazzo* had been able to judge them only by the report of some French friar, since he did not understand our language at all; and he was so content with the excuses I offered on each objection that this Frenchman had left him, that he referred it to my conscience to redress what I would see was in bad taste. I begged him on the contrary to follow the opinion of the man who had made the judgment, admitting in certain things—such as having used the word *fortune,* having named heretic poets, having excused Julian, and the objection to the idea that anyone who was praying should be free from evil impulses at the time; *item,* esteeming as cruelty whatever goes beyond plain death; *item,* that a child should be brought up to do anything, and the like—that that was my opinion, and that they were things I had put in, not thinking they were errors; in other things denying that the corrector had understood my thought. This *Maestro,* who is an able man, was full of excuses for me, and wanted me to realize that he was not very much agreed on this reform; and he pleaded very ingeniously for me, in my presence, against another man, also an Italian, who opposed me.

They kept one of Montaigne's books, a Swiss history in French translation, because the anonymous translator was a heretic and the preface was condemned. A flabbergasted Montaigne rightly concludes that "it is wonderful how well they know the men of our countries."

There was more politeness and consideration about a month later when Montaigne went to take leave of his friendly critic:

On the fifteenth of April I went to say good-by to the *Maestro del Sacro Palazzo* and his colleague, who urged me not to use the censorship of my book, in which censorship some other Frenchmen had informed them there were many stupid things; saying that they honored both my intention and affection for the Church and my ability, and thought so well of my frankness and conscience that they left it to myself to cut out of my book, when I wanted to republish it, whatever I found too licentious in it, and among other things the uses of the word *fortune*. It seemed to me that I left them well pleased with me; and to excuse themselves for having scrutinized my book so attentively and condemned it in certain details, they cited me many books of our time by cardinals and churchmen of very high reputation, which had been censured for a few such imperfections that did not affect in the least the reputation of the author or of the work as a whole. They urged me to help the Church by my eloquence (those are their courteous formulas) and to make my abode in this city, at peace and without trouble from them. These are persons of great authority and potential cardinals.

The kind words might be merely formula, but the experience was pleasant and the thoughtful consideration of his book flattering. If a few official criticisms remained valid, still Montaigne had been defended by this able, learned, responsible younger man whom he obviously liked, and a fine tribute had been paid to his integrity. An amateur in theology, he had come off as well as most professionals under the scrutiny of experts. He had every reason to be well satisfied.

When he returned home late in 1581, he must have been advised almost immediately by his publisher Millanges that his *Essays* had already sold well enough to warrant a second edition. This appeared in 1582, with a few additions. By 1584 there seems to have been a third edition published in Rouen and elsewhere, though no copy of it is now known. A fourth was to appear in Paris in 1587, and the fifth, in three books, in 1588.

The *Essays* were honored in 1584 in two influential works that bore the same title, "French Bibliography." In one, Du Verdier quotes a long extract from Montaigne's essay "Of Books" (II:10). In the other, La Croix du Maine devotes to him a long, intelligent, and laudatory article. Montaigne's works, he says, so abundantly show his great learning and marvelous judgment, and also his varied reading, that there is no need to speak further about this to readers of that fine book that he entitled *Essays.* He mentions the three editions already published—"so well has this work been received by all men of letters"—and gives a perceptive interpretation of the title. He has heard, he says, that some do not set the book as high as it deserves; but he dares to assure, without fear of contradiction by the unbiased, that it is very commendable. And he concludes with a comparison that Montaigne must have liked, though its manner makes the *Essays* seem rather imitative: "And to say what I think of the book in a word, I will say that if Plutarch is so esteemed for his fine works, Montaigne should be for having imitated him so closely, principally his *Moral Essays.* And if Plutarch has been esteemed the only one of the learned whose works should survive (if it happened that all other authors were lost), I say that the man who has followed and imitated him most closely must be the most commendable after him. . . ."

A year earlier (May 23, 1583), one of the most learned men of his time had paid a glowing tribute to Montaigne and his book. The famous Dutch scholar Justus Lipsius wrote to his friend Theodore van Leeuwen (Leewio) that he had told the printer Plantin about the "French Thales," saying that "certainly the like of his wisdom does not dwell among us." The letter was published three years later with a marginal note explaining that Lipsius refers to Michel de Montaigne's French book entitled *Essays,* which he finds "honorable, wise, and very much to his taste." Since Lipsius' letters were widely known and circulated, Montaigne may have known of this judgment well before it was published. Though Lipsius was prone to adulation, this high praise from abroad, so soon, by a great scholar, and by a Latinist for a book in French, was a fine boost for the *Essays.*

From the first the book enjoyed the sincere flattery of borrowings. Matthieu Coignet in his "Instruction for Princes" (1584), Guillaume Bouchet in his "Evenings" (1584), and Montaigne's brother-in-law La Chassaigne de Pressac in "Cleander, or Honor and Valor," which follows his translation of Seneca's *Epistles* (1582), were merely the earliest borrowers; others were soon to follow.

Thus despite some detractors, mentioned by La Croix du Maine and soon to be castigated by the devoted Marie de Gournay, the *Essays* were a success from the first. And although we cannot be sure, it seems very likely that Montaigne learned of each tribute soon after it was paid. If his real originality, the self-portrait, was not always what the reader liked best, still the book was well received by many; and after all, the whole book was a self-portrait. Montaigne, who had found so few kindred spirits in such a corrupt time, who felt truly at home in no group of men of letters, had made real contact with others; his bottle in the sea had come into friendly hands. If he was different from others, the difference was less real than apparent, and certainly no obstacle to communication. The experience of having the *Essays* liked and understood by so many readers added to Montaigne's confidence and to his sense of belonging among others.

MAYOR OF BORDEAUX

New light shed recently by the late Alexandre Nicolaï on Montaigne's election to the mayoralty shows the high probability of the following facts. Since Marshal de Biron's heavy-handedness had for once united Henry of Navarre and his wife Margaret in their indignation, he had to be replaced as mayor by someone with a surer judgment, a more delicate touch. Montaigne's friend and neighbor, the Marquis de Trans, an important member of the great Foix family, was host to the peace negotiators in 1580 at his château of Fleix. It was he who suggested Montaigne's name for the office. All parties concerned—Henry III, Catherine de' Medici, Henry of Navarre, and Margaret of Valois—knew Montaigne and respected his loyalty, moderation and integrity. All agreed, and the loyal *jurats* accepted their decision by electing Montaigne mayor. But Montaigne did not want the position, for he had been hoping for another, more honorable and much less arduous, that of ambassador to Venice.

Certainly in his *Travel Journal* Montaigne shows no elation on receipt of the news. He had written cryptically a week before of news from France that he had been waiting for since four months back. He takes his time about returning, and says he intended to refuse the position until a letter from his king gave him no choice.

Yet even if it was not what he wanted, it was an honor, and one that was to add to his confidence and to draw him still closer toward his fellows. Even his father before him had presumably sought the office; he himself neither had sought it nor wanted it. The Bordeaux Parlement had not recognized his merits; he had not been used adequately at court; his only important negotiation that we know of, honorable though it was, had failed. He often doubted his fitness for any available public service and his chances of being called on. His election as mayor of Bordeaux, unsought and in his absence, was a surprise unappealing but not at all unflattering.

He first heard of it on September 7, 1581, during his second stay at La Villa, two weeks after the worst night he had ever endured. The news came via Rome in letters from Monsieur de Tausin in Bordeaux, dated August 2, and urging him to accept. Five days later he started back leisurely to Rome, found his official notification from the *jurats,* stayed two weeks, and only then returned, expeditiously enough, to France. His reluctance was not caused only by other hopes. He felt old, sick, ill-suited to the job; and he remembered how it had worn down his father. But five days after he reached Montaigne on the last day of November, 1581, he received from his king a polite order to accept:

Monsieur de Montaigne, because I hold in great esteem your fidelity and zealous devotion to my service, it was a pleasure to me to hear that you were elected mayor of my city of Bordeaux; and I have found this election very agreeable and confirmed it, the more willingly because it was made without intrigue and in your remote absence. On the occasion of which my intention is, and I order and enjoin you very expressly, that without delay or excuse you return as soon as this is delivered to you and take up the duties and services of the responsibility to which you have been so legitimately called. And you will be doing a thing that will be very agreeable to me, and the contrary would greatly displease me.

Montaigne's confidence is evident in the way he presented himself to the *jurats*. Candidly he informed his future colleagues just how far he intended to involve himself. Since he thought that they had elected him in honor of his father, he told them that his father had shortened his life in this office and that he would not follow his example, though he admired it. He would lend and not give himself to his job, take it to his mind and judgment and not to his heart and entrails; the mayor and Montaigne would always be two. In modern parlance, he would earn only his own ulcers.

His first two-year term passed fairly quietly. France was enjoying a short respite from open civil war while Spain, the great rival, was occupied with problems in Portugal and the Netherlands. Marshal de Matignon, Biron's successor as the king's lieutenant general in Guyenne, was an able soldier and diplomat who wanted to keep the peace; he and Montaigne worked together splendidly. There was a pleasant moment early in 1582 when the king sent a special court of justice to Bordeaux to rule on cases arising from the last peace treaty. Montaigne made strong friends among the jurists, one of whom, Antoine Loisel, dedicated the closing address to him in a fine tribute. In 1583 Montaigne was reelected, and he apparently accepted this time without constraint. His election was challenged by a rival supported by the Parlement, but it was promptly sustained by the Council of State. Only two men before him had been called to a second term since the office of mayor, after a lapse, had again become elective in 1550; and he took pride in this honor.

The two years of his second term were critical ones for France. The death of the duke of Anjou, last surviving brother of the childless king, on June 10, 1584, made the Protestant leader Henry of Navarre the heir presumptive. Henry III lacked the strength to be either a popular king or a good one, and his support of Navarre as his rightful heir inflamed the resentment against him. The intransigently Catholic League came back to life under the leadership of Henri de Guise, enlisted the ready help of Spain, put forward the old Cardinal de Bourbon as its own pretender, and issued from Péronne a resounding manifesto (March 30, 1585) calling for strong measures against the Protestants. Under its pressure, the king abolished all Protestant rights. The Pope declared that Navarre and Condé had no claim to the succession. France was now torn by three official parties. Soon began the "War of the Three Henrys," only one of whom was to survive.

Meanwhile in Bordeaux Montaigne was active in initiating the reconstruction of the tower of Cordouan in the mouth of the Gironde. Concerned for the people, he and his *jurats* sent a remonstrance to Henry III against the multiplication of tax-free offices, the cost of legal proceedings, and the oppressive weight of taxes on those who could least afford to pay. Much of his activity centered around Henry of Navarre, whose seizure in peacetime of the town of Mont-de-Marsan raised many problems. Navarre's wife Margaret of Valois, repudiated by her brother and then by her husband, came to consult Montaigne as a possible intermediary. Letters to Montaigne from Navarre's chief minister, Duplessis-Mornay, show the high regard in which he was held and mention direct correspondence between him and the king. In the tension after Anjou's death, Montaigne wrote to Navarre's mistress, his old friend Corisande d'Andoins de Gramont, urging her to guide her lover wisely in his best interests and those of France. His advice was effective, for it was echoed in her letters to Navarre and in Henry's policy. In December of the same year (1584) Montaigne entertained the future Henry IV at his manor with some fifty of his knights and their attendants, and then had a stag started in his forest to keep them busy two days more.

In 1585, after the Péronne Manifesto, the tension grew extreme in Bordeaux. Almost daily letters to Matignon show Montaigne's tireless vigilance and alertness to head off dangers to his city, whether from Vaillac and his Leaguists in the Château Trompette that dominated the town or from unruly Protestant soldiers in the vicinity. When it became necessary, he backed up Matignon stoutly in having Vaillac and his men ousted from their fortress. When an armed review of all the townspeople was due and Montaigne's colleagues thought it best to limit the ceremonial volleys and to play safe, he argued instead that the safest and wisest course was to show full confidence in the troops by appearing openly as though there were no danger and letting the salvos resound as usual. The result was typical of Montaigne's mayoralty: nothing happened for history to record. But planning, judgment, and courage had produced that result.

At the end of his second term, the plague was raging almost unchecked in the city. Few people remained, among them a skeleton Parlement and two *jurats* out of seven. Outsiders were not allowed to enter. The time came for the departing mayor to turn over his office formally to his successor. Montaigne was away at the moment, as he often had to be; he asked the remaining *jurats* if he could not just as well meet them outside the city for this ceremony; they readily agreed; and so he did what seemed wise, and stayed out of town. Three centuries later he was to be blamed for this. But his contemporaries offered no criticism that we know of, and he does not even mention the matter in defending his mayoralty. It has seemed to many later writers that it would have been heroism to return. To Montaigne this would almost certainly have seemed to be inconsistent and false heroics.

In the summer of 1586, after about a year at home on his *Essays,* he went through a trying period when a large League army was besieging Castillon a few miles away. A moderate among extremists, he was battered by both sides, by the League soldiers on the one hand and by Protestant freebooters on the other. Then the plague spread to his neighborhood, and for six months he had to guide his family in flight around the country before he dared return to his manor and his *Essays.*

Looking back on his mayoralty in his book, Montaigne feels a need to defend himself—not for his conduct but for his wholly unorthodox attitude, for his refusal to engage himself completely. He has been criticized for it, he says, but undeservedly so.

> I did not leave undone, that I know of, any action that duty truly required of me. . . .
>
> It is acting for our private reputation and profit, not for the good, to put off and do in the public square what we can do in the council chamber, and at high noon what we could have done the night before, and to be jealous to do ourselves what our companion does as well. . . .
>
> I did not have that iniquitous and rather common disposition of wanting the trouble and sickness of the affairs of this city to exalt and honor my government; I heartily lent a shoulder to make them easy and light. Anyone who will not be grateful to me for the order, the gentle and mute tranquillity, that accompanied my administration, at least cannot deprive me of the share of it that belongs to me by right of my good fortune. And I am so made that I like as well to be lucky as wise, and to owe my successes purely to the grace of God as to the intervention of my own action.

Montaigne knew that those who really were acquainted with his work were aware of its worth. The two Henrys, Matignon, the *jurats,* the people in general—their faith gave him confidence; and the work itself had shown him that in the melee of political administration during a dangerous period he could act decisively and well. In the process, his concern and fondness for the people had grown. The Remonstrance to the King (August 31, 1581) by the mayor and *jurats* protests against all the exemptions from taxes enjoyed for various reasons by the rich, since "it is very reasonable that those who have greater means should feel the burden more than those who live only precariously and by the sweat of their body"; and against the venality and multiplication of judicial offices, "whereby the poor people suffers greatly. . . . The poor, not having the means to meet so many expenses, are most often constrained to abandon the pursuit of their rights." It asks further that the official almoners be obliged to take care of the growing number of persons reduced to beggary by the terrible costs of the wars.

For all the poverty and inequity, the citizens of Bordeaux are a good people, as Montaigne writes later. His natural languor, he says, must not be taken as a proof of impotence, "and still less of insensibility and ingratitude toward this people, which used all the utmost means it had in hand to please me, both before they knew me and after, and did even more for me by giving me my office again than by giving it to me in the first place. I wish them all possible good, and certainly, if the occasion had arisen, there is nothing I would have spared for their service. I bestirred myself for them just as I do for myself. It is a good people, warlike and idealistic, capable nevertheless of obedience and discipline and of serving some good purpose if it is well guided."

Montaigne had come a long way from his humanistic disdain for the vulgar. Earlier he had admired isolated common folk, cannibals, foreigners, nearly always paradoxically and a little perversely; now he showed real affection for his own common people, the plain citizens of Bordeaux. Nor did he come to like the mighty less for liking the humble more; on the contrary, working with them gave him much more insight into their problems. Power he still saw—as well he might in France in the late 1580s—as a corrupting force; his main allegiance, sympathy, and even admiration went more and more to the simple people; but his good will was not restricted to any class. Before the trip, the individuals and groups with whom Montaigne felt real solidarity had been the exception; now they were the rule, and the exceptions were few. Beneath the unnatural surface diversity of human folly, he now found a natural unity in bedrock human nature, and drew from it the sense of solidarity of a man who really belongs.

THE PEASANTS AND THE PLAGUE

These six important years spent in the world held yet another lesson for Montaigne. As he wandered with his family in flight from the plague, he was amazed at the natural simple bravery of the unlettered country folk whom he saw dying like flies all about him. The late *Essays* are colored and warmed by the experience.

Montaigne's concern with humble folk goes back virtually to his cradle. His father, we remember, had had him held on the baptismal font by simple villagers standing as godparents, and then nursed by others of the humblest class, in order to bind him to the people, to those who might need his help. Montaigne says that the scheme worked pretty well; though it may be significant that he makes no such statement until after the experience that we are coming to. Most of his early remarks in praise of the common folk are paradoxes to shame the learned. When he excepts the people from his attack in the "Apology," it is as an inferior antagonist "that is not aware of itself, that does not judge itself, that leaves most of its natural faculties idle."

In the ten years following the "Apology," Montaigne tells of seeing in the civil wars some amazing exhibitions of courage by peasants under torture—mainly, to be sure, to protect their money, but also for religion. He notes that in people of low social rank "it is not so new to see some trait of rare goodness," whereas among the rich and noble "examples of virtue rarely lodge." He finds that "The souls of emperors and cobblers are cast in the same mold . . . they are led to and fro in their movements by the same springs as we are in ours."

Montaigne's admiration for the peasants he saw during the plague fills the important chapter "Of Physiognomy" (III:12). We are so in love with artifice, he begins, that we do not properly appreciate Socrates. Socrates talked naturally and simply, like a peasant or a woman; his examples were drawn from our commonest actions; everyone understood him. He aimed not at vain fancies, but to give us the understanding that really is useful for life. Always the same, he rather lowered than raised himself to the earthy plane of the greatest human wisdom and brought out the greatest effects of the human soul. Humble people are wise in the same natural way:

> To what end do we go mobilizing ourselves with these efforts of learning? Let us look on the earth at the poor people we see scattered there, heads bowed over their toil, who know neither Aristotle nor Cato, neither example nor precept. From them nature every day draws deeds of constancy and endurance purer and harder than are those that we study with such care in school. How many of them I see all the time who ignore poverty! How many who desire death, or who pass through it without alarm and without affliction! This man who is digging up my garden, this morning he buried his father or his son. The very names by which they call diseases relieve and soften their harshness: phthisis is the cough to them; dysentery, looseness of the bowels; pleurisy, a cold; and according as they name them mildly, so also they endure them. Diseases must be something very serious to interrupt their ordinary work; they take to their beds only to die.

When the heaviest blows of the civil war struck, the people suffered greatly. They were pillaged of everything, Montaigne says, even of hope, and he with them. But the sternest test for all was the plague:

> Now what example of constancy did we not see then in the simplicity of this whole people? Each man universally gave up caring for his life. The grapes remained hanging on the vines, the principal produce of the country, as all prepared themselves, indifferently, and awaited death this evening or the next day, with face and words so little frightened that it seemed that they had made their peace with this necessity. . . . I saw some who feared to remain behind, as in a horrible solitude; and I found in them normally no other care than that of burial. . . . In short, a whole nation was suddenly, by practice, placed on a level that concedes nothing in firmness to any studied and deliberated resoluteness.

It is these brave and simple peasants who completed Montaigne's change from the philosophy of apprehension to a relaxed and contented confidence in human nature:

> It is certain that to most people preparation for death has given more torment than the dying. . . . If you don't know how to die, don't worry; nature will tell you what to do on the spot, fully and adequately; she will do this job perfectly for you; don't bother your head about it. . . . We trouble our life by concern about death, and death by concern about life. . . . It is not against death that we prepare ourselves . . . we prepare ourselves against the preparations for death. . . .
>
> I never saw one of my peasant neighbors start cogitating about the countenance and assurance with which he would pass this last hour. Nature teaches him not to think about death except when he is dying. And then he has better grace about it than Aristotle, whom death oppresses doubly, both by itself and by such a long premeditation. . . . Isn't that what we say, that the stupidity and lack of apprehension of the vulgar gives them this endurance of present troubles, greater than we have, and this profound nonchalance about sinister accidents to come? . . . For heaven's sake, if that is so, let us henceforth hold a school of stupidity.

From himself Montaigne had learned that natural simplicity can handle pain; from the peasants of Guyenne he now learned that it can handle death as well. Socrates and the peasants are not new exponents of his views; but never before has he been so united with them or so sure of his ideas. An element of criticism and contrast still remains, but it is small. Now Montaigne seems to feel that man in general is on his side and that the fools are the eccentric exceptions. His natural trustfulness and kindliness are now confirmed by his sense of human soundness and unity. It is no accident that the last part of this same chapter, "Of Physiognomy," is full of his good will toward mankind:

> And in truth, I am not very mistrustful and suspicious by my nature; I am prone to lean toward the more favorable excuse and interpretation; I take men according to the common order, and do not believe in these perverse and unnatural inclinations, unless I am forced to by clear evidence, any more than in monsters and miracles. . . .
>
> And I hate no one; and I am so squeamish about hurting that for the service of reason itself I cannot do it. And when chance has summoned me to criminal condemnations, I have tended to fall short of doing justice. . . . To me . . . may apply what they said about Charillus, king of Sparta: "He could not possibly be good, since he is not bad to the wicked." Or else thus . . . "He must certainly be good, since he is good even to the wicked."

Throughout the essays and additions of 1588, Montaigne's sense of human solidarity and unity is complete. He is convinced that every man, common or distinguished, is a true specimen of mankind. Where once he had said that our main task is to live for ourselves, now he finds that to live fully for ourselves we must live somewhat for others. More and more his individual portrait becomes generally human as well. The success of the first *Essays,* the trip, the mayoralty, and the peasants in the plague, all have shown him that many of his strongest attitudes and ideas are shared, practiced, and even taken for granted, by many. In his own eyes long before Emerson's, he has become a truly representative man. His revolt against stoical humanism has been supported; he belongs with mankind in general. The humanization of the humanist is complete.

⸎ 7 ⸎

The Whole Man

1586-1592

THE last years of Montaigne's life were perilous and terrible for a France badly weakened by twenty-five years of civil war and threatened from within and without. Though Henry III favored Navarre as his legitimate heir and urged him to turn Catholic, the pressure of religious feeling made him a reluctant ally of the League. Against these combined forces Navarre had a hard time holding his own. He sought what help he could from Protestant England, Germany, and Switzerland; but it was mainly his brilliant leadership that kept him in the fight and brought his first real victory at Coutras (October, 1587). Then the League overplayed its hand. In effect, Guise held his king captive in insurgent Paris on the Day of the Barricades (May 12, 1588), forced him to flee on the next day, and made him convoke the Leaguist Estates General in December at Blois and submit to most of their wishes. Henry III finally retaliated by having Guise and other League leaders assassinated (December 23). But revolt spread all the faster, until the king had to turn to Navarre for help. As the new allies besieged Paris, Henry III was in turn assassinated (August 2, 1589) by a Parisian monk. Henry of Navarre became Henry IV, the first and only Protestant king of France.

Most of the country, however, was against him, and Mayenne's League armies were still strong. He had to fight shrewdly and furiously. A succession of victories in the north—Dieppe, Arques, Ivry, Rosny—did little more than enable him to hold his own. Once, after a long siege, he came close to taking Paris, but he failed. Finally, after long deliberation and urging, he abjured his Protestantism (1593). More than anything else, this move brought defeat to the League and Spain. In February, 1594, Henry IV was consecrated; in March, Paris opened its gates to him. Though much remained to be done, he was at last master of his kingdom.

Montaigne had fervently hoped to see his king in Paris; but he died a year and a half too soon. After the miserable period that followed his mayoralty, he had returned at last to his hearth and his *Essays*. He must have worked fast to finish the thirteen great chapters of the third book and the five hundred and odd additions to the first two. For he was too important now not to be called on for advice and service.

Three days after the great victory at Coutras, Henry of Navarre was at Montaigne (October 23, 1587) to spend the night for the second time. We have no record of their talk; but there is good reason to believe that Montaigne gave him the advice that he was to follow, not to pursue his advantage by a counterdrive that might seem less like reprisal than rebellion. Three and a half months later, Montaigne, though tired and sick, took the road to Paris (February 10, 1588). A League band held him up on the way, in the forest of Villebois, and robbed him of his money and papers. Barely a week after Montaigne's arrival in Paris, the veteran Spanish envoy, Don Bernardino de Mendoza, was reporting the news to King Philip II (February 25): "Monsieur de Montaigne is a Catholic gentleman serving the man from Béarn [Henry of Navarre] on the instructions of Monsieur de Matignon; and since it is not known who is entrusted with the affairs of the aforesaid man from Béarn, it is suspected that the arrival of this personage is motivated by some secret mission."

Three days later he had more to report:

Monsieur de Montaigne is considered an intelligent man, though a little meddlesome. I am told that he controls the countess de Guiche [Corisande d'Andoins de Gramont]—a lady of great beauty who lives with the sister of the man from Béarn, for she is the latter's mistress—and that he is in relations with that prince. Whence it is deduced that he is coming to accomplish some mission and that the king wants to use him so that he will try, in conjunction with the aforesaid countess de Guiche, to persuade the man from Béarn to agree to what His Majesty wishes.

The League was not yet finished with Montaigne. After following the court in its flight to Chartres and Rouen after the Barricades, he was back in Paris, in bed with the gout, when he was arrested and taken to the Bastille as a hostage at the League's command. The queen mother heard about it promptly, talked to Guise, and had Montaigne released within four or five hours of his arrest.

Montaigne was very ill in Paris, so ill that the doctors feared death and he hoped for it; but he bore it, according to his friend Pierre de Brach, with serene bravery, and was not long inactive. The same Brach helped him see through the presses of Abel L'Angelier the first edition of the *Essays* that included all three books. One of his warmest and most possessive admirers, young Marie Le Jars de Gournay, came to see him in Paris, was accepted as his "covenant daughter," and entertained him more than once at her family's manor in Picardy. Before returning home he followed the court to Blois, where he had a chance to visit with old friends like Pasquier and De Thou.

Even the assassination of Guise did not stop him from working for his king. He took messages to Bordeaux for Matignon, now mayor, and joined in consultations with him there. After the death of Henry III his allegiance went to his lawful successor. A fine letter to Henry IV early in 1590 (January 18) reveals that Montaigne had recently written him more than once and had only now been answered.

He tells Henry that he has always considered him as his future king and hoped for his success "even when I had to confess it to my curate." Henry's victories in the north are serving his cause in the southwest, where Matignon's splendid services may remind the king of Montaigne's assurances and hopes. This summer may make Henry's mastery secure; for popular inclinations go in waves, and he may have started such a wave. Montaigne could wish, however, that the king had restrained his soldiers after the victory in the outskirts of Paris: "To conduct such affairs as you have in hand it is necessary to use uncommon ways. Moreover, it has always been observed that where conquests, because of their greatness and difficulty, could not be thoroughly completed by arms and force, they have been completed by clemency and magnanimity, excellent lures to attract men, especially toward the just and legitimate side. If rigor and punishment occur, they must be put off until after the possession of mastery." In concluding, Montaigne regrets that he has just received Henry's letter of November 30, too late to join him at Tours as instructed. He thanks him for wishing to see "a person so useless, but yours even more by affection than by duty," and ends: "May it be soon in Paris, Sire; and there will be neither means nor health that I will not employ to come."

This and the following letter tell much of Montaigne's manner with the great. Deferent and polite to his king, but frank and firm in advice as man to man, he writes as he lived, "head high, face and heart open."

Later in 1590 (September 2), Montaigne, sick with tertian fever, again answers a letter from his king. On receiving earlier orders, he says, he has written Matignon three times to make an appointment but has had no reply. He still hopes to join Henry and begs him not to think of reimbursing him.

I will never begrudge my purse on the occasions for which I would not want to withhold my life. I have never received any gift from the liberality of kings any more than I have asked it or deserved it; and have received no payment for the steps I have taken in their service, of which Your Majesty has had partial knowledge. What I have done for your predecessors I will do again much more willingly for you. I am, Sire, as rich as I wish to be. When I have exhausted my resources with Your Majesty in Paris, I will make bold to tell you so; and then, if you consider me worth keeping longer in your retinue, I will cost you less than the least of your officers.

Montaigne never did join the king, presumably for reasons of health. He seems to have remained at home, with his mother and his wife, attending to the marriage of his daughter Léonor (May 5, 1590), corresponding with Marie de Gournay, Justus Lipsius, and others, and most of all rereading and correcting his *Essays*. He did not change the thought, but sharpened the style, shortened the sentences. He composed no new essays, but he added over a thousand passages—some of a word or two, others of several pages—which constitute altogether about one quarter of the entire work. On what must have been the leaves of a copy of his 1588 edition he wrote his additions in the margins, working surely and carefully, often leaving several successive versions in his fine small hand. These leaves, rebound, are what we now call the "Bordeaux Copy," the basic text of the *Essays*. On the frontispiece he changed "fifth edition" to "sixth," and wrote a new and final motto; on the flyleaf he set down careful instructions to the printer. Long before, he had written that we must always be booted and ready to go. If death kept him from adding still more to his book, it did not find the book unready.

In his sixtieth year his health went from bad to worse, with throat troubles added to his kidney stone. It was a throat inflammation that finally killed him (September 13, 1592), after leaving him—according to one account—speechless for his last three days. His last words were for his friend Pierre de Brach, with whom he would have liked to talk. He died hearing Mass in his bed.

After his death, through the care of Pierre de Brach, a copy was made of the "Bordeaux Copy" and sent to Marie de Gournay, who had it published in Paris in 1595.

Within the final parts of the *Essays*—Book Three and the additions to the 1580 text—we find none of the major changes and developments that we have observed earlier. Montaigne continues to gain confidence in himself and his convictions, in man and a sort of native human intelligence; and as he does, he grows bolder in expression. There are occasional variations of mood: "Vanity" dwells on man's condition rather ruefully, "Experience" triumphantly. But Montaigne's mind, though not closed, is now fully formed.

Still skeptical in temper and turn of mind, he is yet very sure of many things. Foremost of these is the value of his plan of self-study and self-portrayal. More and more he writes about himself, aware that he will never know all the answers but also that he knows this subject of his better than any other writer ever knew his own. And now he sees the resemblance between men that makes knowledge of self mean knowledge of mankind. Now he sees man as a social being, not merely as an individual. Now he speaks his mind positively about the two matters that are closest to his heart and that fill the final essays—human nature and human conduct.

The essays become longer in Book Three, the titles short. The brief, clearly defined chapter so common earlier now seems to Montaigne constrained and artificial. He has much to say, and everything holds together. His thought does not move naturally in tight categories, and his aim is to show not only the substance of his thought but the movement of it. Most of the new essays deal at some length among other things with Montaigne, with his book, with youth and age.

"The Useful and the Honorable" (Chapter 1) pleads for decency against expediency and shows the problem of ethics in public life. "Repentance" (2) defends Montaigne for rarely repenting by showing that men do not really change much and that true repentance hardly comes except from God. "Three Kinds of Association" (3) treats Montaigne's favorite company —attractive men, attractive women, and books. "Diversion" (4) is shown to be the best treatment for grief, thanks to our inconstancy. "Some Verses of Virgil" (5) deals with sex—its importance in our nature, the need for frankness, the false standard that makes chastity in women (like valor in men) synonymous with goodness. "Coaches" (6) mainly condemns the cruelty of Europeans in the New World. "The Disadvantage of Greatness" (7) explains its subject.

In "The Art of Conversing" (8) Montaigne discusses his favorite occupation and its requirements. "Vanity" (9) is shown to be the essence of man, and Montaigne's love of travel an example. In "Husbanding Your Will" (10) he shows, à propos of his mayoralty, the danger of excessive involvement through ambition. "Cripples" (11) exposes the falsity of many alleged miracles and the evils of witch hunting. "Physiognomy" (12) praises Socrates for the moral beauty and strength of his simple humanity, which even peasants share. And "Experience" (13) discusses the problem of knowledge, to which experience leads more surely than reason; portrays the bodily habits by which experience has allowed Montaigne to live as long as he has; and concludes on the importance of the physical in our makeup and the beauty of life lived in accordance with our nature as a being composed of body and soul.

What is man's nature? How therefore should he live? These are the questions that Montaigne asks himself throughout his final essays. And since proper living depends on our nature, the first question to answer is what we are.

THE NATURE OF MAN

In the early essays Montaigne often seems to question whether there is such a thing as human nature. He sees little but chaos and inconsistency in the individual, little but diversity in the race. His sense of differences in man and men is one of his vitalizing contributions to human psychology; but it makes any generalization virtually impossible.

At the end of his life, however, he finds unity both within each man and in mankind. Having already shown all that education can do for the individual, he now stresses the fact that it cannot do everything:

> Natural inclinations gain assistance and strength from education; but they are scarcely to be changed and overcome. . . . We do not root out these original qualities, we cover them up, we conceal them. . . .
>
> Just consider the evidence of this in our own experience. There is no one who, if he listens to himself, does not discover in himself a pattern all his own, a ruling pattern (*une forme sienne, une forme maistresse*) which struggles against education and against the tempest of the passions that oppose it.

Montaigne still sees more difference than resemblance in mankind, but now he sees both: though our faces, he says, are different enough to tell us apart, they are enough alike to tell us from the animals. He finds that his long self-study has made him a good judge of others, often better able than they to explain their conduct to them. Evidently, his observations have general validity. "I set forth a humble and inglorious life," he writes; "that does not matter. You can tie up all moral philosophy with a common and private life just as well as with a life of richer stuff: each man bears the entire form of man's estate."

Montaigne's sense of kinship and solidarity now extends, more seriously and less paradoxically than in the early essays, to many large groups: the people of the New World, foreigners in general, the populace of Bordeaux, freaks, and women. Now he senses, and fully shares, a broad strain of common humanity.

For Montaigne, the basic fact of man's nature is that he is made up of body and soul. And his basic deduction is that these two are equal parts.

Most moral philosophy since Plato, and much before, considers the soul a likelier candidate for immortality than the body, and therefore the better of the two. Often it carries this preference further and regards the soul as good, the body as bad; or further still, and calls the body the prison of the soul. Christian doctrine is generally more balanced, believing as it does in the ultimate resurrection of the body, which is the gift and the temple of God. When Montaigne mentions the Christian attitude, it is in this vein.

Montaigne's emphasis on the body is not new in the late essays. "It is not a soul," he had written earlier, "it is not a body that is being trained; it is a man; these parts must not be separated." He had rejected Plato's doctrine of the immortality of the soul on the grounds that to separate our two main parts thus is the death and ruin of our being. Now he writes that there is nothing in us purely either corporeal or spiritual, and that wrongly we tear apart a living man. "To what purpose," he asks, "do we dismember by divorce a structure made up of such close and brotherly correspondence?" Again and again he reminds us of the importance of the body, which we tend to forget or ignore. Man's condition, he writes, is wonderfully corporeal; likewise life is "a material and corporeal movement, an action imperfect by its very essence, and irregular." For the same reason he warns that since our life is part folly, part wisdom, whoever writes about it only reverently and regularly leaves out more than half of it.

The body as Montaigne sees it is simple, earthy, solid, sane, slow to change. It appears to be entirely subject to nature, in which it is fortunate; for nature makes even pain contribute by contrast to its pleasure and places its greatest pleasures in the satisfaction of its needs. The body can sometimes even help the soul by giving it stability.

The soul is very complex and infinitely powerful for our good or ill. Centrifugal, erratic, never at rest, it is always trying to improve on nature and succeeds only in making us miserable. Properly directed, however, it can do wonders.

Its parts or functions are not always clear. The mind (*esprit*) sometimes represents the entire soul, sometimes its knowing and reasoning function. The imagination is the most flighty part of the soul, undiscerning between truth and falsehood, often needing consolation from the mind. Reason (*raison*) has at least two distinct meanings or aspects for Montaigne—that of *reasoning,* which is rash, plausible, and dangerously irresponsible, and that of *reasonableness,* which is excellent. Understanding (*entendement*) and judgment, which are virtually synonymous, test new appearances by comparing them with present and past evidence and then assign them the appropriate degree of truth or falsehood, good or evil. Judgment is the master quality, of which conscience appears to be one function. Where judgment rules the soul harmoniously, all will be well; where it does not, mind and soul are dangerous even to their possessor.

Located within us, the soul, or mind, has no direct contact with externals. It receives the reports of the senses on the impacts that objects make on them and tries to find the truth from these reports. In this it has no assurance of success, since it accepts things always in its own fashion. But this same arbitrariness gives it infinite power for our happiness.

> Things in themselves may have their own weights and measures and qualities; but once inside, it [the soul] allots them their qualities as it sees fit. . . . Health, conscience, authority, knowledge, riches, beauty, and their opposites, are stripped on entry and receive from the soul new clothing, and the coloring that it chooses . . . and which

each individual soul chooses. . . . Each one is queen in its realm. Wherefore let us no longer make the external qualities of things our excuse; it is up to us to reckon them as we will. Our good and our ill depend on ourselves alone.

Since the soul is so powerful, it should help the body, as Montaigne had seen earlier. In particular it should protect man against the tyranny of age. Montaigne's body was hard for his soul to control in his youth because it was lusty; now the reverse is true: "This body flees irregularity and fears it. . . . It dominates in its turn, and more roughly and imperiously. . . . I defend myself from temperance as I formerly did from sensuality. . . . Wisdom has its excesses, and needs no less moderation than folly." For our apparent reform in old age is really a decline, a "cowardly and rheumatic virtue" produced by sourness and weakness; we do not really abandon our vices but only change them, usually for the worse. If Montaigne is to be master of himself as he wants, his mind must combat this deformation: "Let it grow green, let it flower meanwhile, if it can, like the mistletoe on a dead tree." His body, he tells us, is often depressed; his soul, when it is not actually blithe, is at the very least tranquil and cheerful. If his body were as governable as his soul, he would be well off indeed.

Since the soul deceives the senses even as it is deceived by them, it may exercise its power through pleasant delusion. No matter; the point is that it has the power:

The body has, except for a little more or less, only one gait and one bent. It [the soul] is diversifiable into all sorts of forms and adapts to itself, and to its condition, whatever this may be, the feelings of the body and all other accidents. Therefore we must study and investigate it, and awaken in it its all-powerful forces. There is neither reason, nor prescription, nor force which has power against its inclination and its choice. Of so many thousands of biases that the soul has at its disposal, let us give it one suitable for our repose and preservation, and we are not only safe from all injury but even gratified and tickled, if it seems good to it, by injuries and evils.

It makes its profit from everything indiscriminately. Error, dreams serve it usefully as a lawful means to place us in security and contentment.

All this, of course, is vanity: the senses gullible, the soul deceptive and irresponsible, the body decadent from youth, disobedient to the soul and rivaling it in importance. This is a far cry from the usual bright Renaissance picture of man as the little universe, the microcosm.

Moreover, vice comes as naturally to us as vanity. Ambition, jealousy, envy, vengefulness, superstition, despair, cruelty—the seeds of these are inborn, and to destroy them would be to destroy the fundamental conditions of our life. However, we also have it in us to recognize vice and control it. To know it is to hate it; repentance follows it as the night the day. Thus although vice is important, vanity remains the keynote: "I do not think there is as much unhappiness in us as vanity. . . . We are not so much full of evil as of inanity."

Vanity is not a new idea to the author of the "Apology for Raymond Sebond." He merely argues it now better and oftener, making it a theme of most of the essays of Book Three.

It is man's wisdom, not man's follies, he writes in "Three Kinds of Association," that makes him laugh. Is there anything except us in nature, he asks in "Diversion," that feeds on inanity and is controlled by it? "Some Verses of Virgil" treats the vanity of our physical makeup. The whole world revolves about the urge for copulation, which we call love; yet no other action so comically reveals us as the plaything of the gods. "Husbanding Your Will" shows mostly vanity in public affairs and the motives that drive us into them; "Cripples," our love of the vanity of speculation and dispute; "Physiognomy," the vanity of artificial reason and knowledge, which do us more harm than good as defenses against the fear of pain and death. Finally, "Experience" finds vanity in our very essence: "I who boast of embracing the pleasures of life so assiduously and so particularly, find in them, when I look at them thus minutely, virtually nothing but wind. But what then? We are all wind. And even the wind, more wisely than we, loves itself for making a noise and moving about, and contents itself with its own functions, without wishing for stability and solidity, qualities that do not belong to it."

Vanity is the heart as well as the title of Chapter 9. Montaigne admits that there is vanity in his love of travel. "But where," he asks, "is there not? And these fine precepts are vanity, and all wisdom is vanity. 'The Lord knoweth the thoughts of the wise, that they are vain.' " Vanity is a part of our condition, and a large part at that. There may be little that we can do about it, but at least we should know it. Montaigne's conclusion is particularly eloquent:

> If others examined themselves attentively, as I do, they would find themselves, as I do, full of inanity and nonsense. Get rid of it I cannot without getting rid of myself. We are all steeped in it, one as much as another; but those who are aware of it are a little better off—though I don't know. . . .
>
> It was a paradoxical command that was given us of old by that god at Delphi: "Look into yourself, know yourself, keep to yourself. . . . It is always vanity for you, within and without; but it is less vanity when it is less extensive. Except for you, O man," said that god, "each thing studies itself first and, according to its needs, has limits to its labors and desires. There is not a single thing as empty and needy as you, who embrace the universe: you are the investigator without knowledge, the magistrate without jurisdiction, and all in all, the fool of the farce."

Our essence, then, is vanity. But the equation works both ways. Vanity is our essence; and we are fools if we despise our essence. Montaigne had attacked this malady of self-disdain earlier, and now, in the chapter on vanity itself, he returns even harder to the attack.

To be sure, we must recognize our vanity, our great limitations. We are very physical, very variable, often comical, something less than omniscient. To ignore this is to invite arrogance, presumption, and self-disdain, dangerous faults but easily curable. But at the same time we must recognize our possibilities, which are richly adequate for living. The little learning that we need to live at ease is in us; and if we cannot find it by ourselves, Socrates will teach us how. His greatest service was precisely that of showing all that human nature can do by itself. We may not even need his help if we look within us as Montaigne does, and try to become authorities not on Cicero but on ourselves. "In the experience I have of myself," Montaigne writes, "I find enough to make me wise, if I were a good scholar." The best cure for our vanity, indeed for all our errors—anger, inconstancy, ignorance, bad judgment, and all the rest—is not to read about them in books but to see them, truly and steadily, in ourselves. It is not really at our own expense, as he had written earlier, that we become wise in this way; it is only at the expense of our self-conceit. "Let us only listen: we tell ourselves all we most need."

These are the main facts of human nature for Montaigne. Our limitations are great, but our resources for living well are greater. If we look into ourselves, we shall find them.

THE JOY OF LIVING

In all man's limitations and all his resources Montaigne finds tremendous possibilities for happiness or unhappiness, for good or evil, for wisdom or folly. These pairs of opposites are closely related. Happiness produces neither goodness nor wisdom, though it is favorable to them; goodness produces happiness but not wisdom; wisdom produces both goodness and happiness and depends on neither. Thus wisdom is basic. The surest way to seek goodness and happiness is through wisdom.

Perhaps, indeed, it is the only way. Only a miraculous intervention of God, Montaigne believes, can make radical changes in our intellect or morals. By ourselves we cannot force our "ruling pattern" or extirpate our vices. However, we can control these by a wise use of our virtues. The essence of a good education is not to impose on us "right" ways of thinking and acting but to train our judgment to make us wise, and therefore good, with a wisdom and a goodness that is our own. We should "know how to do all things and like to do only the good." Only such free choice has moral meaning.

Wisdom, for Montaigne, consists entirely in knowing how to live. This involves four things: knowing ourselves, accepting ourselves and our life, learning what to expect of ourselves, and learning our duty to ourselves and others. Here the basic element, on which all the others depend, is self-knowledge. Ethics must be firmly rooted in psychology: what we should be, in what we are. Acceptance is equally necessary. For unless we accept as well as know ourselves, with our strengths and our weaknesses, we will expect too much or too little of ourselves, and in either case fall short of our best possible moral effectiveness. And unless we accept life with its joy and its pain, we will fall into the vice of sourness and ingratitude.

The last two parts of wisdom guide us in our main responsibility here on earth, namely our conduct. To do what is fitting and best we must first know what is fitting and best. To know this for ourselves alone is not easy; to know it for others as well is still harder. But the challenge is as rewarding as it is difficult.

For Montaigne this is the only way to seek real goodness. As long as there is inner strife, we cannot be entirely good, and we fall short of the ideal. Judgment, the voice of wisdom in us, must rule within; but it rules by persuasion, so that our whole selves join in our action. Only a soul in harmony with itself can be wholly good. Integration is a condition of integrity.

The most difficult thing is to know what we owe to ourselves and to others. Montaigne's final conviction of this is a measure of his growth. In the early years of his retirement, as we have seen, he had called it the greatest thing in the world to know how to belong to oneself. Now his sense of solidarity makes him reject this ideal as one-sided and incomplete. The problem is to belong to oneself and to the human race as well. Its most obvious aspect is the question to what extent public service is a duty.

"I am of this opinion," Montaigne now writes, "that the most honorable occupation is to serve the public and be useful to many." However, in the next breath he adds that he himself abstains from this partly from laziness, partly from conscience. At first glance his paradox seems perplexing. But actually laziness is not an important motive. What Montaigne probably means is simply that he loathes the lack of freedom of public life and knows that his loathing could be called laziness. His real reason for turning his back on a way of life that he admires is the difference between the norm and the rarely attained ideal. He finds that vices are necessary to hold the state together; that the general welfare may demand at any time that a public person do evil, sacrificing the honorable to the useful. Rare are the men who, like Epaminondas or Montaigne's father, can keep their integrity in public office.

> Public life must have relation to other lives. The virtue of Cato was vigorous beyond the measure of his time; and for a man who undertook to govern others, a man dedicated to the public service, it might be said that it was a justice, if not unjust, at least vain and out of season. . . .
>
> The virtue assigned to the affairs of the world is a virtue with many bends, angles, and elbows, so as to join and adapt itself to human weakness; mixed and artificial, not straight, clean, constant, or purely innocent. . . . He who walks in the crowd must step aside, keep his elbows in, step back or advance, even leave the straight way, according to what he encounters. He must live not so much according to himself as according to others, not according to what he proposes to himself but according to what others propose to him, according to the time, according to the men, according to the business.

Plato says that anyone who escapes with clean breeches from handling the affairs of the world escapes by a miracle.

In other words, in public we can live neither as we like nor even as good a life as we like. This is where conscience motivates Montaigne's abstention. If he had to, he feels, he could adapt himself to public life; but he would rather not. The more he has experienced it, the more he is disgusted with it. He is better at private life, he thinks, as well as happier. Let those who are happier—and presumably no worse—in public life do their own dirty work.

"Husbanding Your Will" (III:10), whose subject is Montaigne's mayoralty, goes to the heart of the larger question of duty to self and to others. In a way that Pascal was to remember when he wrote on diversion, Montaigne analyzes the motives that drive most people out of themselves, whether into public office or elsewhere, and finds mainly ambition and a sort of centrifugal force bred of emptiness, laziness, and bad conscience. As importunate to themselves as they are serviceable to others, most men seek business simply for the sake of being busy. They do so with a good conscience, since everyone accepts uncritically the notion that public life is intrinsically altruistic, private life intrinsically selfish. But this notion is false. Self-abdication need not be self-abnegation, nor self-possession selfishness. We must remember our principal duty. "The principal responsibility that we have," Montaigne insists, "is to every man his conduct; and that is why we are here. . . . You have plenty to do at home within you; don't go away."

No longer will complete withdrawal do for Montaigne: "He who lives not at all with respect to others (*à autruy*)," he now writes, "hardly lives with respect to himself (*à soy*)." But the opposite is equally foolish and unnatural: "Just as anyone who should forget to live a good and saintly life, and think he was quit of his duty by guiding and training others to do so, would be a fool; even so he who abandons healthy and gay living of his own to serve others therewith, takes, to my taste, a bad and unnatural course."

The ideal balance lies in proper self-possession, which means lending but not giving ourselves to others. Its opposite, self-abdication, Montaigne finds ineffective and often bad: ineffective when we let our work possess and control us instead of controlling it; bad when we abdicate our judgment, reason, and conscience in favor of our passions or those of others. Then we become mere partisans, obliged upon command to distort the features of truth and goodness. Our judgment must see the good with the bad in the enemy, the bad with the good in our own side; it must distinguish the mask from the face, the mayor from Montaigne. Constructive moderation, so badly needed in violent times, comes not from passion but only from self-possessed loyalty.

Proper self-possession in general lies in a delicate balance of conflicting duties. It would be fairer and better for man, Montaigne believes, if he consciously included himself in applying the golden rule. His argument rests not on hedonism but on justice. Excessive self-devotion defeats itself; but excessive self-abnegation, however admirable (like that of Montaigne's father as mayor), is also unjust. The true point of justice, Montaigne believes, is to contribute all fitting duties and services to society, but with the aim of applying our experience to our own lives. We owe friendship not only to others but also to ourselves: not a false friendship that drives us to frantic pursuit of false goods such as glory, learning, riches; nor an overindulgent one that breaks down our character as the ivy does the wall it clings to; but "a salutary and well-regulated friendship, useful and pleasant alike." The true point of this friendship is difficult to find but all-important, a secret mystery of the temple of Pallas. "He who knows its duties and practices them . . . has attained the summit of human wisdom and of our happiness."

Montaigne sometimes calls goodness easy, because it follows nature instead of resisting it; sometimes he seems to call it hard, to combat the common illusion that public life is harder than private. In public, he says, we play a part, wear a mask, display our "art"; in private we reveal ourselves, our own face, our "nature." In private we need the reality of goodness, which is character; in public we need only its semblance, which is personality. It is easier to simulate goodness than to practice it.

Moreover, the incentive of glory makes public life easier. It is a brilliant thing to win a battle, to conduct an embassy, to govern a people. It is a rarer matter, more difficult, and less noticeable, to be pleasant and just with ourselves and our household, not to let ourselves go, not to be false to ourselves. Thus, despite popular opinion, private lives accomplish duties as harsh and strenuous as other lives, or more so. Moreover, private goodness is more appropriate and important than public: "Alexander's virtue seems to me to represent a good deal less vigor in his theater than does that of Socrates in his humble and obscure activity. I can easily imagine Socrates in Alexander's place; Alexander in that of Socrates, I cannot. If you ask the former what he knows how to do, he will answer: 'Subdue the world'; if you ask the latter, he will say: 'Lead the life of man in conformity with its natural condition'; a knowledge much more general, more weighty, and more legitimate."

Since our *raison d'être* is our conduct, private life is our proper function and domain. To live it well is the greatest masterpiece of all.

We are great fools. "He has spent his life in idleness," we say; "I have done nothing today." What, have you not lived? That is not only the fundamental but the most illustrious of your occupations. "If I had been placed in a position to manage great affairs, I would have shown what I could do." Have you been able to think out and manage your life? You have done the greatest task of all. . . . To compose our character is our duty, not to compose books, and to win, not battles and provinces, but order and tranquillity in our conduct. Our great and glorious masterpiece is to live appropriately.

In order to perform this masterpiece, we must recognize and accept ourselves as children of nature. From the "Apology" and "Cannibals" to "Physiognomy," Montaigne continues to insist on this point. We belong in nature, but we will not admit it. In our reckless attempts to improve on her by art, we have lost her track; we have changed her into all sorts of forms, as perfumers do with oil, so that we no longer recognize her in ourselves and must seek her in simple people or animals. We have been fools to abandon a guide who led us so happily and so surely.

Nature helps us in every way. She uses our inconstancy to divert our grief; gives us better laws than our own, since she knows her business better than we do; makes pain serve pleasure, and our needs pleasant to satisfy; teaches us how to die, and in fact all we need to know to be content. She is a sweet guide, but no more sweet than prudent and just; we cannot fail if we follow her, and the more simply we follow her the better.

Artificiality is our undoing. Foolishly we take its glister for gold. Sometimes—and here Montaigne speaks from personal experience—we let it spoil our lives. We beset ourselves with all sorts of fears, like that of death, which may not even be natural; we give ourselves more trouble in preparing for death than we would in dying; we make death the goal of life instead of merely the end. For all her grateful children nature takes care of these things better than ever we can and on a moment's notice.

From the refusal to accept ourselves as children of nature comes presumption and its offspring, the wildest of our maladies, self-disdain. Because we think of ourselves as above and apart from the order of creation, we cut our obligations to fit a higher being than ourselves, and so order ourselves to be necessarily at fault. We like to think that the higher our aim, the higher will be our attainment. But Montaigne disagrees, like Socrates, whose motto, "According as one can," he often borrows. Our nature, he finds, simply does not work that way: constant failure, however inevitable, makes us give up trying, either through discouragement or through too easy acceptance of the inevitable. There is the danger also that it will make us actually worse; for our normal impulse to cover up perhaps a minor vice will add to it the ugly vice of hypocrisy. "Between ourselves," Montaigne writes, "these are two things that I have always observed to be in singular accord: supercelestial thoughts and subterranean conduct. . . . They want to get out of themselves and escape from the man (*eschapper à l'homme*). That is madness: instead of changing into angels, they change into beasts; instead of raising themselves, they lower themselves."

In Montaigne's eyes this is perhaps our greatest folly: to want to escape from man's condition. It is not natural but purely man-made, a product of our erratic mind. We would be wiser, happier, and better, he insists, to accept ourselves as we are, to let our conscience be content with itself not as the conscience of an angel or of a horse but as the conscience of a man. Self-knowledge is the road to this acceptance: "We seek other conditions because we do not understand the use of our own, and go outside of ourselves because we do not know what it is like inside."

For self-study reveals our resources to us as well as our limitations. Socrates, whose principal rule was "Know thyself," can help us to see them. Whereas the peasants are a good corrective, he is a perfect model and guide. He has shown human nature how much it can do by itself; he can teach us the little learning that we need for happy living. Beyond these resources, which are natural, all others are practically vain and superfluous. By our usual standard of values, which sets art above nature, the simplicity of Socrates is low and backward. With relish Montaigne points up the paradox by portraying him in these terms:

> He was always one and the same, and raised himself, not by sallies but by disposition, to the utmost point of vigor. Or rather, he raised nothing but rather brought it down and back to its original natural point. . . .
>
> By these vulgar and natural motives, by these ordinary and common ideas . . . he constructed not only the most regulated, but the loftiest and most vigorous beliefs, actions, and conduct that ever were. . . . See him plead before his judges. . . . There is nothing borrowed from art and the sciences; the simplest recognize their means and their strength; it is not possible to go back further and lower.

Thus in Montaigne's opinion the paradox works both ways. By trying to escape man's condition and be angels, men become beasts. By accepting his lot, humbly and simply, as a child of nature, Socrates became the best man that ever lived. Acceptance such as his is a condition of goodness.

Even the preceding remarks, however, show that for Montaigne self-acceptance alone is not enough; a measure of self-improvement is also needed. The peasants are good, or at least innocent; but Socrates is perfect. He has improved himself, as they presumably have not, by applying his reason to his natural resources. Their goodness is primarily natural; his is fully human.

Montaigne is often at odds with himself—verbally at least—on the question of self-improvement. It is no wonder that his moral countenance has appeared to different readers as anything from earnest reformer to complacent hedonist. Often it is his love of sally and paradox, humor and irony, that leads him into inconsistency of statement; but there are other reasons, too. In respect to himself, frankness makes him say that he has sought to be better, and perhaps in some measure succeeded; but frankness and modesty make him regard this measure as small. Moreover, he considers self-acceptance bad in excess but good in moderation: in excess the enemy of self-improvement, in moderation the condition of it. Since most people put all the emphasis on self-improvement, Montaigne usually stresses his lack of it. "I have not corrected, like Socrates," he writes, "my natural dispositions by force of reason. . . . I let myself go as I have come, I combat nothing." What virtue he has, he calls a sort of accidental innocence.

Yet even in this same context, while saying that he has restricted his vices too little, he admits that since they aid and abet one another, he has kept them apart and confined, as isolated and simple as he could. Such statements seem more candid than the others and closer to the center of his thought. Without boorish conceit he could not claim much more than he does when he says that he has put all his efforts into forming his life. And still more revealing is a later comparison of himself with the stoics: "What they did by virtue; I train myself to do by disposition (*complexion*)."

The somewhat surprising use of the term *complexion* (as something trained and acquired) is a result of Montaigne's conception of the mechanics of self-improvement. It is through habit, he finds, that wisdom works to produce goodness. Habit is all-important, all-powerful; a second nature, as Aristotle says, and no less strong than the first. Virtue can work by fits and starts, and in that way we can do almost anything. But what we really are we are constantly, by habit. One of the reasons why Montaigne sets Socrates so high is that by habit he had made his goodness a second nature. When Montaigne trains himself to do well by disposition, he is following what he considers the best way to be good and the only way to be really and wholly good.

For we can improve on nature, good and strong as she is. Our native state seems to be a sort of balance of conflicting elements: the vices on the one hand, and on the other hand conscience and repentance. As we grow, either side may prevail, or neither. Education can do much but not everything; we may control, but we cannot extirpate, our natural propensities. Reason will normally tell us to follow nature, but not always; when it does not, it is reason we must follow.

Montaigne's main hope of human betterment lies in an inborn seed of universal reason. Although he is sincerely religious, the Protestant experience and the religious wars apparently make him feel that religion has failed as a moral stimulus, presumably because it has not allowed enough for human limitations. With his intense practicality, he cares hardly at all for belief, almost exclusively for individual and civic morality. The one passage where he speaks his mind clearly on this matter is worth quoting at length:

> Shall I say this in passing: that I see held in greater price than it is worth what is almost alone practiced among us, a certain idea of scholastic probity, slave to precepts, held down beneath fear and hope? What I love is the kind that laws and religions do not make but perfect and authorize, feeling in itself enough to sustain itself without help, born in us of its own roots from the seed of universal reason imprinted in every man who is not denatured. This reason, which straightens Socrates from his inclination to vice, makes him obedient to the men and gods who command in his city, courageous in death not because his soul is immortal but because he is mortal. It is a ruinous teaching for any society, and much more harmful than ingenious and subtle, which persuades the people that religious belief is enough, by itself and without morals, to satisfy divine justice. Practice makes us see an enormous distinction between devoutness and conscience.

Just as Montaigne rejects nature as the arbiter of our morals, so he rejects religion as their base. He dislikes its constraint, its self-seeking motivation by fear and hope. He not only accepts us as neither horses nor angels, he does not want us to be anything but men. He seems to feel that in giving us reason to help us rise above mere nature, God has put us quite on our own to be fully ourselves.

In the early essays, doubtful of our ability to become good, Montaigne had mainly urged us to be natural. Now he still urges that, but most of all he wants us to be human.

Our vices, for example, he regards as natural but not human. Most of those that he hates worst—disdainful treatment of social inferiors; contempt for the body and its rights; eagerness to make others sad by our misery; lying, disloyalty, mob violence, torture, cruelty—he clearly connects, by statement or suggestion, with inhumanity.

Meanwhile his highest praise for ideas, actions, or men is to call them human. The philosophical opinions he likes best are, he says, "the most solid, that is to say the most human and the most our own." An honorable man will not lie, for he wants to be seen just as he is inside, where "either all is good, or at least all is human." Epaminondas deserves a place among the best of men because even in the sternest of actions he exercised goodness and humanity. Even for a god the term is high praise: Vulcan's generosity to his unfaithful wife Venus is "of a humanity truly more than human." And the concept is central in Montaigne's statements of his ideal: "The most beautiful lives, in my opinion, are those that conform to the common human pattern. . . . There is nothing so beautiful and legitimate as to play the man well and duly."

To be natural and yet naturally to surpass the rest of nature; to accept ourselves and yet by the means God has given us to improve ourselves: this for Montaigne is to be truly human.

For all his stress on the need of accepting the limitations imposed on us by nature, Montaigne wants no others. Truly representative of his age, his ideal is to live not only simply but also as richly and fully as possible. Already before 1580 he had recommended versatility in his essay on education when he advised that a young man should be able to do all things and do good only from free choice. In the late essays he stresses this value even more and also treats a new aspect of it—the problem of encroaching age.

He fears aging, as we have seen, as a diminution. "I hate that accidental repentance that old age brings," he writes. "I shall never be grateful to impotence for any good it may do me. . . . Miserable sort of remedy, to owe our health to disease!" He held these views in youth as in age. Now that his sluggish body drags him down, his mind must fight to stay green. Man, he feels, must strive to be limited by neither youth nor age. The ideal is to be whole.

Montaigne's main praise of versatility in general is in "Three Kinds of Association" and "Experience." Versatility is close to his ideal of simplicity in that it usually means the ability to relax as well as be tense, to move and act happily and gracefully on lower social and intellectual levels than one's own. "The fairest souls," he writes, "are those that have the most variety and adaptability."

Here again, habit is the great power that makes us what we are. The great danger is that it will enslave us to our usual ways and spoil us for varied living. It can also be used, however, to make us and keep us adaptable: "I would admire a soul with different levels, which could be both tense and relaxed, which would be well off wherever its fortune might take it, which could chat with a neighbor about his building, his hunting, and his lawsuit, and keep up an enjoyable conversation with a carpenter and a gardener."

Praise of this ability to relax graciously fills much of the conclusion of Montaigne's last chapter. In the midst of great wars, he tells us, Caesar and Alexander found time to enjoy natural pleasures, and Brutus to make notes on Polybius. For all their severity, both Catos accepted and enjoyed our human bondage to Venus and Bacchus. Epaminondas and Scipio the Elder spent pleasant hours singing and playing with youngsters. Socrates again is our best model. Courageous, noble, patient and self-restrained in every sort of hardship including death, he could lose himself in some beautiful thought for hours at a time yet could also drink the rest of the army quietly under the table when that was in order, or play gracefully and happily with children at their games. Such rich versatility is wholly admirable. "We should never tire of presenting the picture of this man as a pattern and ideal of all sorts of perfection."

Thus the main components of Montaigne's ethical ideal meet in Socrates—the natural simplicity of self-acceptance, the human virtue of self-improvement, the rich versatility of a life lived fully on all levels. His was life at its best, fully and purely human.

"It is an absolute perfection and virtually divine to know how to enjoy our being lawfully (*loyallement*)." Thus Montaigne, almost in conclusion, attempts, not for the first time, to compress into a formula the heart of his message. It is a reminder that we should accept ourselves and life and live appropriately; it is also a statement that the proper enjoyment of our being is a form of perfection.

Montaigne had not always felt and talked in this way. On the contrary, until his illness he had even mistrusted life. Paradoxical, but only in its Epicurean extremeness, is his bleak statement from the "Apology": "Our well-being is only freedom from being badly off. . . . To have no pain is to have the most good that man can hope for. . . ." But now his confidence makes him contradict this view when he adds: "I am glad not to be sick; but if I am sick, I want to know that I am; and if I am cauterized or incised, I want to feel it. Truly, if anyone rooted out the awareness of pain, he would extirpate at the same time the awareness of pleasure, and in the end would annihilate man. . . . Evil is a good to man in its turn. Neither is pain something for him always to flee, nor pleasure for him always to follow."

This is the second of the two important concepts that give Montaigne confidence in life. To the arbitrariness of the soul he has added, apparently since his illness, the interdependence of pleasure and pain. Now he finds life full of contrasts which our soul must learn to accept and to harmonize: "Our life is composed, like the harmony of the world, of contrary things, also of different tones, sweet and harsh, sharp and flat, soft and loud. If a musician liked only one kind, what would he have to say? He must know how to use them together and blend them. And so must we do with good and evil, which are consubstantial with our life. Our existence is impossible without this mixture, and one group is no less necessary for it than the other." Naturally, we will prefer pleasure to pain and encourage it, but we will regard both sanely and accept them as necessary elements of our life. They are not completely pure; there is pain in pleasure and pleasure in pain. To live well and happily we must use them wisely, like the musician in the passage above: "They are two fountains: whoever draws from them the right amount, from the right source, at the right time, whether city, man, or beast, he is very happy."

It takes attention to exercise this artistry in living, but it is a pleasant and rewarding occupation. Montaigne enjoys life twice as much as others, he believes, for enjoyment depends on application. As the life that remains to him grows shorter, he works to make it deeper and fuller. We must study, savor, and ruminate our joys, he finds, in order to be properly grateful to him who grants them to us.

The basic condition is acceptance: of ourselves, our condition, and our life, with all the limitations and possibilities that nature has placed in them. We are not to reject, like some, the natural pleasures of the body, for to do so is to reject our condition; we are to accept them not avidly but simply and gratefully. Nor are we in effect to cast life aside by always seeking to "pass the time"; it is too precious to be allowed to slip through our fingers. It is Montaigne's grateful and gracious acceptance of all that human life means that gives such happy and steady serenity to his comments on the pains and drawbacks of his declining years: "If I had to live over again, I would live as I have lived. I neither regret the past nor fear the future. . . . I have seen the grass, and the flower, and the fruit, now I see the dryness—happily, since it is naturally."

Montaigne's earlier friends the stoics had also believed in the goodness of life; but the difference in the underlying reasoning is complete. They started, in effect, by accepting the belief in a supreme and good intelligence that governs the universe for the best. Thus what seems a particular evil must be in reality a good; and if we are to be wisely in tune with nature, we must learn to accept it as good and call it that. Montaigne's conviction carries weight because it is not at all a preconception. Though his Christian God is all-good and all-powerful, he is too remote to play a part here. Montaigne's optimism is the fruit of his meditations on a life rich in experience, painful as well as pleasant.

> As for me, then, I love life and cultivate it just as God has been pleased to grant it to us. I do not go about wishing that it should lack the need to eat or drink . . . nor that we should beget children insensibly with our fingers or our heels, but rather, with due respect, that we could also beget them voluptuously with our fingers and heels. . . . Those are ungrateful and unfair complaints. I accept with all my heart and with gratitude what nature has done for me, and I am pleased with myself and proud of myself that I do. We wrong that great and all-powerful giver by refusing his gift, nullifying it, and disfiguring it. Himself all good, he has made all things good.

It is the long meditative journey Montaigne has traveled that gives power and persuasion to his final triumphant hymn of gratitude. The critical apprehensive early stages, summed up in the famous "Que sçay-je?" had led to deep self-examination. Self-examination, trial by illness, and experience have led at last to confidence in self, in man, and in life. For the final stages and the journey as a whole, Montaigne's final motto is the true one: "*Viresque acquirit eundo*—He acquires strength as he goes."

Conclusion

MONTAIGNE'S meditative journey may be, and has been explained in various ways, its different aspects groupe around various concepts. Much of it can be centered around hi favorite moralists, books, and systems. Yet what he takes fron them is what he chooses; even in his beloved Socrates there is mucl that he rejects. These pages have tried to show as central his neec his quest, and his discovery of confidence in man and in life.

His early apprehension was rooted in pessimism about life an man's power to endure its pains bravely. Even his early revolt wa partly pessimistic, in that he doubted whether most people coul live up to the standards of stoical humanism. But his abandonmen of his early attitude was motivated not only by mistrust of it bu also by trust in his own resources. From that moment on he con tinued to discover new resources in himself, in life, and in man.

The growth of his confidence in himself and in life is seen readil enough if we contrast the final chapters, "Physiognomy" and "Ex perience," with such early ones as "The Taste of Good and Evil, "To Philosophize is to Learn to Die," and "Solitude." It is cleare still in the contrast between the remarks just quoted, "Our well being is only freedom from being badly off" and "Himself all gooc he has made all things good."

The same chapters reveal the growth of his confidence in mar This is perhaps clearest, however, from his use of certain term: Even as late as "The Education of Children" he defines his idea man as a *gentilhomme;* later the term becomes the more demc cratic *honneste homme.* And his words for the common people–

vulgaire, commun, peuple, populaire—change from forms of disdain to forms of praise. Though his irony and humor must make us cautious in assessing his comments, it is striking that these are almost all unfavorable in the early essays, favorable in the late.

Before 1580, even when he grants that common people are often brave and good, he marvels to find these qualities in "the crude herd," "this soft and effeminate mob." He classes them with children for their gullibility, deplores the "brutish stupidity" of their thoughtlessness of death, and censors their cruelty in victory. In the "Apology" he disdains even to attack their opinions, since these are beneath contempt. He calls their conduct base and vile. He contrasts them again and again with the learned, the wise, the excellent minds. He finds "more distance than between heaven and earth" separating the sages that he seeks to emulate from "the mob of our men, ignorant, stupid and asleep, base, servile, full of fever and fright, unstable and continually floating in the tempest of the various passions that push and drive them; depending entirely on others."

After 1580 Montaigne has almost no criticism of the *vulgaire*. At what may be his frankest he recognizes a difference between his kind and theirs, but only to stress the importance of talking their language: "If we disdain to adjust ourselves to low and vulgar souls—and the low and vulgar ones are often as well-regulated as the subtler ones (all wisdom is foolish that does not adapt itself to the common unwisdom)—we should no longer meddle with either our own affairs or those of others: both public and private affairs are worked out with these people." After 1580, Montaigne places them generally on the side of nature. Socrates drew on the most vulgar and natural actions and motives to build up the finest, sanest, and strongest life and philosophy ever. For nature's traces still remain on "this rustic mob of unpolished men." If it is stupidity that makes them so brave, then we had better cultivate it.

There is irony in all this, to be sure; but Montaigne's irony is clear and carefully directed. There is a semantic change, too; for Montaigne's favorite *vulgaire* of the late years is the peasants who live closest to nature. But it is with common people in general that he now identifies himself—and proudly: this is the great change. He is "of the common sort," he now writes twice—once to add, "except in that I so consider myself." His life is "common and private," his soul "low and common," his condition "mixed, crude," his thoughts and conduct "low and humble." Now the term *vulgaire* often seems almost synonymous with *human;* and we have seen what praise that is. Now he uses the term to contrast his own wisdom with the rigor that he has rejected: "Whoever cannot attain this noble stoical impassibility, let him take refuge in the lap of this plebeian (*populaire*) stupidity of mine."

The best example of Montaigne's new attitude is the remark with which this book begins. Early in the first version of the "Apology," speaking of how easily the minds of *le vulgaire* can be changed, he had observed: "and practically everybody is of this sort." In his final revision he simply crosses this out. But much later in the chapter he also adds the remark that seems really to replace it, since the vein and the context are the same: "and we are all of the common herd."

Though the vein is the same, the difference is great. Though it is a sally, now it is *we,* not they; now it is all mankind, of which Montaigne is proud. In defining mankind as the *vulgaire,* he also defines the *vulgaire* as mankind. This equation of the herd with humanity is the final step in Montaigne's greatest evolution. The humanist is now fully humanized.

Nor was Montaigne alone affected by his change. More than anyone else, he incarnated and effected the transformation of humanism into *honnêteté.*

He uses this term only in the late essays, never to define it but always to apply it to the kind of person he likes and admires. He says he is grateful to the *honnestes hommes* who have enjoyed his book; it would be good to travel and share ideas with one of them; he hopes that his book may help him to meet one who might be another good friend. The men he likes best to converse with, whose talk can be frank, gay, friendly, and judicious, are of the rare type known as "honnestes et habiles hommes." The word most clearly embodies his final ideal when he uses it of peasants and philosophers alike, demands adaptability of an *honneste homme,* and contrasts the versatility of such a man with the limitations of the courtier.

The ideal of the *honnête homme* was one of Montaigne's most important legacies to the age that followed. Though there were many other sources—Castiglione and Guazzo, to name only two—he was the principal one. Though his ideal, in the hands of others, presently became somewhat more polished and less blunt, more social and less inward, he remained a preponderant influence and a perfect model. When Pascal found *honnêteté* inadequate and turned against it, the man he chose to combat as its strongest champion was Montaigne.

Three of his essays in particular appealed to seventeenth-century readers. In the social chapters, "Three Kinds of Association" and Pascal's favorite, "The Art of Conversing," they enjoyed his reasonableness and adaptability, his capacity for seeing and honoring views other than his own, and his freedom from obstinacy, prejudice, and passion. "The Education of Children" was an even greater favorite, revealing as it did Montaigne's dislike of pedantry and dogmatism; his love of reason, judgment, moderation, and versatility; his cosmopolitanism; his independence of mind and taste. The very way in which he presented himself throughout his book, as a whole man and not simply as an author, was much enjoyed and admired.

If the ideal of *honnêteté* did not attract precisely the same type of people as humanism had earlier, the difference was not great.

Moreover, such difference as there was betokened a cultural change in which Montaigne played a great part. By insisting that humanism be broadly humane, he moved its center of gravity from the scholar to the intelligent man in general.

When humanism spread from Italy to France, it had become what one critic calls a narrow scholasticism, no longer in contact with man and reality. In fear of the reproach of Epicurean impiety it had lost warmth, grace, naturalness, and humanity and had contracted into stoicism. Even while rejecting it in its old constricted form, Montaigne breathed human life into it, enriched it as he enriched his own personality, and in effect revived it under a new name. He summoned it to a new and fruitful task: to understand man, his place in the universe, and—consequently—the way in which he should live.

We may still call him a humanist in his late years. If we do, however, we are in fact declaring that he has changed the meaning of the term. He has given it a breadth and scope it had never had before. He has made it, even as he has made himself, fully human.

Notes

Notes

THE AIM of these notes is to be as brief and as useful as possible. The nature of the book demands careful support of the quotations and paraphrases from Montaigne; and the lack of any one outstanding edition in French has made it seem wise to give page references for three editions in French and one in English. To compensate for this, however, there is a maximum of abbreviation. Page references are normally not given for quotations from short essays or for second allusions to passages already located. Since most of the books referred to were published in Paris, the place of publication is not listed for these. Many old authors are quoted not from the original but from trustworthy modern texts which are more accessible.

No special bibliography has seemed necessary. The best one now available in French is in the article on Montaigne in the *Dictionnaire des lettres françaises: XVIe siècle* (Fayard, 1951). In English, the article in David C. Cabeen's forthcoming *Critical Bibliography of French Literature: Sixteenth Century* (Syracuse: Syracuse University Press) promises to be the best. The writer is much indebted to most of the students of Montaigne mentioned below, and also to the historians on whom he has leaned the most: Henry Lemonnier and J.-H. Mariéjol for Parts 1 and 2 of Volume V and Part 1 of Volume VI of Ernest Lavisse's *Histoire de France* (Hachette, 1911) and Henri Hauser and Augustin Renaudet for Volumes VIII–IX of Louis Halphen and Philippe Sagnac's *Peuples et civilisations: Histoire générale* (Alcan, 1929–33).

The choice of French editions of reference for Montaigne has not been easy. The Municipal Edition of the *Essais* by Fortunat Strowski and others (5 vols.; Bordeaux: Pech, 1906–33) would be ideal if it were more accessible. Conversely, the modern Garnier edition by Maurice Rat in three volumes (1941–42) is readily available and generally good but lacks Villey's clear and unobtrusive indications of the strata of the

Essays, which are always valuable, and indispensable for any chronological study. The three editions that have been used here are those which seem best to combine convenience and completeness with availability. They are the following:

1. Pierre Villey's second, octavo edition (3 vols.; Alcan, 1930–31). Not as widely diffused as the other two, but ideal for the studious reader.

2. Albert Thibaudet's one-volume edition in the Pléiade series (Gallimard, 1934, 1102 pp.). Excellent, handy, widely diffused. If the publisher had not reprinted this in 1950 with an altered pagination (1274 pp.), this would probably be by now *the* edition from which to quote Montaigne.

3. Jean Plattard's edition in the series Les Textes Français (6 vols.; Roche, 1931–33; reprinted with the same pagination by the Société Les Belles Lettres, 1946–48). Not as rich or convenient as the other two but available and good.

For the reader who prefers to take Montaigne in English, the most accurate translation and by far the best edition is that of Jacob Zeitlin (3 vols.; New York: Knopf, 1934–36). Though this is the English edition of reference in this book, the translations given here are my own. Some have appeared already in the Classics Club volume, *Selected Essays of Montaigne* (New York: Black, 1943), and in the Crofts Classics edition, *Selections from the Essays of Montaigne* (New York: Crofts, 1948).

All page references to the *Essays* are given in the Notes for all four of these editions in the following order. First the book number (in Roman capitals) and chapter number (Arabic) from the *Essays* (II:12); next the page number in Villey, whose three volumes correspond to Montaigne's three books; then a capital A, B, or C, to designate (after Villey) material written by Montaigne in time to appear in the editions of 1580, 1582, and 1587 (A), in that of 1588 (B), or after 1588 (C). Then follow the page references to the other editions: Plattard's, introduced by a capital P and the volume number; Thibaudet's (Pléiade), preceded by a capital T; and Zeitlin's, introduced by a capital Z. No volume references are needed for the last two, since the first is in one volume, and the other (like Villey's) in three volumes that correspond to Montaigne's books.

Thus the second note—II:12, 475A; P:III, 353; T:557; Z:234—means that the passage was written before 1587 and is found in Book II, Chapter 12 of the *Essays;* in Villey's 1930–31 edition, II, 475; in Plattard's, III, 353; in Thibaudet's, p. 557; in Zeitlin's, II, 234.

Nearly all the (A) material was written before 1580. Here and there in the editions of 1582 and 1587, however, Montaigne made minor changes in his text that are not listed in our four editions of reference to avoid swamping the reader with notes that would often be trivial. In the present study, the importance of Montaigne's development before 1580 makes it imperative to quote exactly what he wrote then, even if a later change is small. Where such changes occur, the text in this book is translated from the two-volume edition by Dezeimeris and Barckhausen (Bordeaux: Gounouilhou, 1870–73), which reproduces the 1580 edition of the *Essays* and the variants of 1582 and 1587; and the fact is indicated by an added reference to this edition, in this fashion: II:12, 319–320A; P:III, 233–234; T:474; Z:152. Cf. DB:II, 82–83.

Montaigne also changed after 1588 some passages that first appeared at that date. But the chronology of his thought in these final years is less important. Therefore, at the risk of inconsistency, it has seemed better to spare the reader the indications of these changes.

Finally, Montaigne's other writings are quoted from the following editions, which seem the best and most easily available.

Travel Journal: from *Journal de voyage en Italie,* ed. Charles Dédéyan (Société Les Belles Lettres, 1946). Since there are other good editions and an English translation by E. J. Trechmann, passages are identified by date and place as well as by page, in the following manner: *JV*: 164; Rovereto, Oct. 29, 1580.

Letters, dedicatory prefaces, and inscriptions on Beuther's *Ephemeris historica:* from *Œuvres complètes,* ed. Armaingaud (12 vols.; Conard, 1924–41), Vol. XI. Page references are not given for the Beuther because dates are sufficient and also because it may be consulted even better in Jean Marchand's excellent facsimile edition, *Le Livre de raison de Montaigne sur l'"Ephemeris historica" de Beuther* (Compagnie Française des Arts Graphiques, 1948).

Translation of Raymond Sebond entitled *Théologie naturelle:* from *Œuvres complètes,* ed. Armaingaud, Vols. IX–X.

The numerals appearing at the beginning of each note refer to the corresponding pages in this book; the italicized words following the numerals refer to the specific passage on which the note has bearing.

INTRODUCTION

3. *Rabelais . . . Goths.* Rabelais, *Pantagruel,* Ch. 8, in *Œuvres complètes,* Pléiade ed. (Gallimard, 1941), p. 226.

3. *Thus it is . . . a weathercock.* II:12, 475A; P:III, 353; T:557; Z:234.

4. *I would willingly . . . or guessed.* II:1, 20A; P:III, 16; T:325; Z:7. III:9; 399B; P:VI, 62; T:953–54; Z:187.

Ellipses are indicated here in the normal manner (three or four dots) except for one type: those that would represent (A) material added to the 1580 text in 1582 or 1587. In this detail as in others, we have "corrected" the (A) text of the editions of reference by the Dezeimeris and Barckhausen edition.

4. *conflicting epithets . . . equally well.* II:1, 15–16BC; P:III, 13; T:323; Z:5.

4–5. *Yet even . . . medieval theologian.* André Gide, *Essai sur Montaigne* (Schiffrin, 1929); Marc Citoleux, *Le Vrai Montaigne, théologien et soldat* (Lethielleux, 1937).

The question of Montaigne's religion is still debated, but the evidence for his sincerity is much the stronger and continues to gain. The best book on the subject is Maturin Dreano, *La Pensée religieuse de Montaigne* (Beauchesne, 1936). There are very good discussions by Zeitlin in the Introduction and Notes of his edition and by Marcel Raymond in "Attitude religieuse de Montaigne," in *Génies de France* (Neuchâtel: La Baconnière, 1942), pp. 50–67. A more recent survey by the present writer is the article, "Did Montaigne Betray Sebond?" *Romanic Review,* XXXVIII (December, 1947), 297–329.

6. *This view or a variant.* Villey's position is of course much more complex than this; but in application, as in his editions, this is about what it amounts to.

8. *I am nearly . . . radical change.* II:17, 652–53A; P:IV, 85; T:644; Z:321. III:2, 52B; P:V, 37; T:785; Z:21. See below, p. 142.

10. *I want . . . my mutations.* II:37, 850A; P:IV, 227; T:735; Z:409. Cf. DB:II, 327.

10. *Since then . . . cannot say.* III:9, 361C; P:VI, 34; T:934; Z:168.

1: THE YOUNG HEDONIST

12. *Though Montaigne . . . not involved.* The best books on Montaigne's life are Paul Bonnefon, *Montaigne, l'homme et l'œuvre* (Bordeaux: Gounouilhou, 1893); Jean Plattard, *Montaigne et son temps* (Boivin, 1933); and Fortunat Strowski, *Montaigne, sa vie publique et privée* (Nouvelle Revue Critique, 1938). There is much valuable material in Dreano. Alexandre Nicolaï has illuminated certain aspects in *Montaigne intime* (Aubier, 1948) and *Les Belles Amies de Montaigne* (Dumas, n.d. [1950]); and posthumous works of his on *Les Grands Amis de Michel de Montaigne* and *Michel de Montaigne dans la politique* are promised. The *Bulletin des Amis de Montaigne,* which has appeared sporadically since 1913, contains many useful articles, including Nicolaï's "Les Grandes Dates de la vie de Montaigne" (1948–49, pp. 24–66). In English, Zeitlin is always good. The main original sources are the *Essays,* Montaigne's letters and *Travel Journal,* and his family record book, a copy of Michael Beuther's *Ephemeris historica.*

13. *Two or three . . . became Protestants.* Two are certain, Montaigne's brother Beauregard and his sister Jeanne de Lestonnac (the elder). Another sister, Léonor, may have been converted also; Strowski says so (*Montaigne, sa vie publique et privée,* p. 19), but Dreano seems to differ (*Pensée religieuse de Montaigne,* pp. 40–46). Cf. Zeitlin, I, xix.

13. *a real jail of captive youth.* I:26, 317C; P:II, 37; T:176; Z:146. The last part of this chapter, "Of the Education of Children," is our best source on Montaigne's early upbringing and schooling. See also II:8, 133C; P:III, 96–97; T:380; Z:61.

14. *M. de Moneins . . . demeanor.* I:24, 245–47B; P:I, 181–83; T:142–43; Z:112–13. Cf. Strowski, *Montaigne, sa vie publique et privée,* pp. 36–37.

14. *In 1554 . . . able to change.* On Montaigne in the Parlement de Bordeaux, see especially Dreano, Strowski, and the manuscript *Registres secrets du Parlement de Bordeaux* at the Bibliothèque Nationale and the Bibliothèque Municipale de Bordeaux. See also *Essays,* I:23, 219–20A; P:I, 163–64; T:130–31; Z:101. I:25, 265–66A; P:I, 196; T:152; Z:121–22. II:12, 461–64AB, 499–501A; P:III, 342–45, 371–72; T:549–51, 569–70; Z:227–29, 246–47. III:1, *passim.* III:10, 477B; P:VI, 118; T:993–94; Z:226. III:11, 493–94B; P:VI, 129–30; T:1001; Z:233.

III:12, 559–60B; P:VI, 177–78; T:1033–34; Z:264. III:13, 564–78BC; P:VI, 180–90; T:1035–42; Z:265–72.

15. *entangled in . . . for the moment.* II:17, 600A; P:IV, 48; T:618; Z:296.

15. *It is positively . . . once a year.* See especially Nicolaï, "Les Grandes Dates de la vie de Montaigne," *Bulletin des Amis de Montaigne* (1948–49), pp. 24–66.

16. *it was still school.* I:26, 336A; P:II, 51; T:186; Z:154.

16. *When this came . . . to Protestantism.* Strowski, *Montaigne, sa vie publique et privée,* pp. 18–20; Dreano, *Pensée religieuse de Montaigne,* pp. 40–45.

17. *Consider the form . . . right reason.* III:13, 573–78BC; P:VI, 187–90; T:1039–42; Z:270–72.

17–18. *loves to give . . . idleness, freedom.* III:9, 371C; P:VI, 42; T:940; Z:174. Cf. III:13, 600B; P:VI, 207; T:1053; Z:284.

18. *Almost equally . . . at twenty.* II:17, 622–23AC, 634–35AB; P:IV, 63–64, 72; T:629–30, 635; Z:306–7, 312. III:2, 60–64BC; P:V, 43–46; T:789–91; Z:24–26. III:5, 214–15B; P:V, 153; T:863–64; Z:99. III:8 276B; P:V, 198; T:893; Z:128. III:10, 437B; P:VI, 89; T:973; Z:206–7. III:13, 599–603BC; P:VI, 206–9; T:1053–55; Z:283–85.

18. *He takes . . . inclinations.* II:11, 190–94ABC; P:III, 137–40; T:408–11; Z:86–89. III:12, 552B; P:VI, 172; T:1029–30; Z:260.

18. *Rather gay . . . sadness.* I:20, 157A; P:I, 117; T:100; Z:71. II:8, 108A; P:III, 78; T:366–67; Z:48. II:17, 619AB; P:IV, 61; T:627–28; Z:305. III:8, 310B; P:V, 222; T:910; Z:145.

18. *He is lively . . . in the process.* III:13, 645–46BC; P:VI, 239–40; T:1076–77; Z:306.

18. *once, when . . . his character.* See below, p. 25.

18. *Though not an . . . of books* II:17, 626–27A; P:IV, 66; T:631; Z:308–9. II:33, 799–800A; P:IV, 191; T:711; Z:385. III:3, 90BC; P:V, 64; T:803; Z:38. III:9, 416–17B; P:VI, 75; T:963; Z:196.

18–19. *He is neither . . . communicative.* III:3, 78B; P:V, 55; T:797; Z:32–33. III:9, 396C, 405B; P:VI, 60, 66; T:952, 957; Z:186, 191.

19. *Altogether . . . firm vigor.* II:17, 621A; P:IV, 62; T:628; Z:306.

19. *Not a big . . . variety.* I:14, 110–17BC; P:I, 82–87; T:77–81; Z:50–53. I:21, 177AC; P:I, 132; T:110; Z:81–82. I:37, 446C; P:II, 128; T:235–36; Z:204. II:17, 601A, 616–19AB; P:IV, 48, 59–61; T:619,

626–28; Z:296, 303–5. III:2, *passim*. III:6, 237B; P:V, 169; T:874; Z:109. III:9, 408B; P:VI, 69; T:959; Z:192. III:13, 627–28B; P:VI, 226–27; T:1067; Z:297–98.

19. *His attitude . . . their husbands.* II:8, 131–35A; P:III, 95–98; T:379–81; Z:60–62. II:35, 820A and *passim;* P:IV, 207; T:721; Z:395. III:3, 76–77B, 85BC; P:V, 54–55, 60; T:796–97, 800–801; Z:31–32, 35–36. III:5, 188BC and *passim;* P:V, 133; T:850; Z:85.

19. *The several . . . dedicates to women.* "Of the Education of Children" (I:26), to Diane de Foix, comtesse de Gurson; "Twenty-nine Sonnets of Etienne de La Boétie" (I:29), to Madame de Gramont, comtesse de Guissen (or Guiche; better known as Diane or Corisande d'Andoins); "Of the Affection of Fathers for Children" (II:8), to Madame d'Estissac; "Of the Resemblance of Children to Fathers" (II:37), to Madame de Duras. A fifth essay, "Apology for Raymond Sebond" (II:12), is clearly addressed to an unnamed lady who is very probably Margaret of Valois. For details on these ladies, see Nicolaï, *Les Belles Amies.*

19–20. *In his youth . . . legitimate function.* I:55, 603B; P:II, 243–44; T:307; Z:276–77. II:12, 470–72A; P:III, 350–51; T:554–55; Z:232. III:3, 82B, 84BC; P:V, 58–59; T:799–800; Z:34–35. III:5, 217B; P:V, 155; T:865; Z:100. III:13, 606B; P:VI, 211; T:1056–57; Z:287.

20. *Altogether . . . mask of pleasure.* II:11, 193A; P:III, 139; T:410; Z:88. II:12, 470–72A; P:III, 350–51; T:554–55; Z:232. III:2, 61–64BC; P:V, 43–45; T:789–91; Z:25–26. III:13, 582B; P:VI, 193–94; T:1044; Z:275.

20. *In this business . . . no folly.* III:5, 216B; P:V, 154; T:864; Z:99.

20–21. *Besides judgment . . . in his duration.* I:20, 157–58A; P:I, 117–18; T:100; Z:71–72.

21. *Such is . . . he has known.* II:17, 655A; P:IV, 87; T:646; Z:322.

22. *That La Boétie . . . to Montaigne.* A third poem, addressed to Montaigne and a mutual friend, Jean de Belot, deals mainly with La Boétie's heartsickness over the state of France and his wish to leave and settle in the New World. See La Boétie, *Œuvres complètes,* ed. Paul Bonnefon (Bordeaux: Gounouilhou, and Paris: Rouam, 1892), pp. 207–13, 225–35. For a French translation, see *Bulletin des Amis de Montaigne* (1921), pp. 343–80.

The friendship appears in La Boétie's account just as it will in Montaigne's. In a year, he says, it has become perfect; few others in history are even comparable; it will not be forgotten. Based on love and virtue, it enriches both men. Later Montaigne was to call La Boétie the better friend of the two; here his friend gives that honor to him.

23. *Though Montaigne . . . immersed in it.* Note Montaigne's remark about being ignorant of Venus; his admiration for his chaste father, whom La Boétie holds up as a model; and his request that if he must give up married women, his friend lead him to a brothel. Here, in his love poems, and in Montaigne's dedication of his sonnets (*Essays* I:29), La Boétie seems to have had more premarital experience than his younger friend.

24. *Memoir concerning . . . January 1562.* Published by Paul Bonnefon in *Revue d'histoire littéraire de la France* (1917) and in book form (Bossard, 1922).

24–25. *Two actions . . . of his character.* See Strowski, *Montaigne, sa vie publique et privée*, pp. 62–64; Dreano, *Pensée religieuse de Montaigne*, pp. 135–39.

25. *against . . . La Boétie.* II:6, 86–87A; P:III, 64; T:357; Z:39.

25. *Our main view . . . La Boétie's works.* Montaigne, *Œuvres complètes*, XI, 165–88.

26–27. *But two . . . abode of the blest.* Montaigne, *Œuvres complètes*, XI, 176–77.

28. *For two years . . . various amours.* III:4, 102–3B; P:V, 72–73; T:808–9; Z:43–44.

28. *Then, partly . . . by comparison.* III:5, 132–38B; P:V, 93–97; T:821–26; Z:56–61.

28. *But for him . . . contrary directions.* III:9, 399B; P:VI, 62; T:954; Z:187.

29. *If a copy . . . flesh and blood.* III:5, 120B; P:V, 84; T:816; Z:51. Cf. III:9, 394–95BC; P:VI, 58–59; T:951; Z:185.

29. *Eighteen years . . . real pain.* The *Travel Journal* is good authority, for it was never intended for publication. (*JV*:288; La Villa, May 11, 1581.)

29. *To the sage . . . he was alive.* III:4, 104B; P:V, 73; T:809; Z:44. Cf. text and note of II:8, 129; P:III, 93; T:378; Z:58–59.

29. *The influence . . . apprehensive humanism.* Two able writers on characterology, René Le Senne in his *Traité de caractérologie* (Presses Universitaires, 1945), pp. 438, 471, 480–82, and Gaston Berger in his *Traité pratique d'analyse de caractère* (Presses Universitaires,

1950), pp. 101–97, deny Montaigne the emotivity that his friendship shows. But their reading of him leaves out masses of important negative evidence.

2: THE APPREHENSIVE HUMANIST

31. *In these first . . . law and order.* See Strowski, *Montaigne, sa vie publique et privée,* pp. 54–56.

31. *And in December, 1567 . . . troops.* See Dreano, *Pensée religieuse de Montaigne,* pp. 140–41; Strowski, *Montaigne, sa vie publique et privée,* p. 64.

32. *It has even . . . brother at that.* Nicolaï, *Montaigne intime,* pp. 75–77. A strange contract, dated May 23, 1569, is the main evidence for this assumption and is hard to explain otherwise. Montaigne's brother Saint-Martin often wore a gold chain, which was found after his death in the coffer of Montaigne's wife. Montaigne's mother claimed it, and it was restored to her by written contract. Other evidence may be found in Nicolaï's book.

32. *Montaigne's translation . . . father died.* Most of these facts are drawn from the early pages of the "Apology for Raymond Sebond" (*Essays* II:12).

33. *Montaigne showed . . . the author's claims.* Joseph Coppin was the first to show these facts and their importance in *Montaigne, traducteur de Raymond Sebon* (Lille: Morel, 1925).

33. *Many explanations . . . "Natural Theology."* For fuller discussion see D. M. Frame, "Did Montaigne Betray Sebond?" *Romanic Review,* XXXVIII (December, 1947), 297–329.

33–34. *His father's death . . . (October 5, 1573).* See Dreano, *Pensée religieuse de Montaigne,* pp. 141–42; Beuther's *Ephemeris;* and Nicolaï, "Les Grandes Dates de la vie de Montaigne," *Bulletin des Amis de Montaigne* (1948–49), p. 32. Elsewhere (*Les Belles Amies,* p. 115) Nicolaï attributes Montaigne's second honor to 1571 but does not give his evidence. The first mention of Montaigne with this title in "Les Grandes Dates" is dated October 5, 1573.

34. *which was terrible in Guyenne.* Pierre Villey, *Les Sources et l'évolution des "Essais" de Montaigne,* 2d ed. (Hachette, 1933), II, 59–61. Montaigne's discouragement at the times shows, before the *Essays,* in his dedicatory prefaces to La Boétie's works (*Œuvres complètes,* XI, 196–97, 200, 210).

34. *In 1561 . . . was to kill him.* II:37, 860–61A; P:IV, 234–35; T:740–41; Z:413–14. The dates that Montaigne gives on his Beuther (*Œuvres complètes,* XI, 274, 276–77) suggest 1562 as the year that his father fell ill.

34. *Now that Montaigne . . . worry him.* Apparently from 1568 to 1573, judging by I:14, 110–16B; P:I, 82–87; T:77–81; Z:50–53. Villey, *Les Sources et l'évolution,* II, 420, takes the voyage that freed Montaigne from money worries to be that of 1580–81. But the 1588 edition (see Strowski's phototypic edition, Hachette, 1912, Plate 47) said that he was in this anxious state four or five years; and it presumably began with his father's death.

34. *In the same . . . a reminder.* II:6, 83–93A; P:III, 61–69; T:355–60; Z:37–42.

34. *When these examples . . . the throat?* I:20, 153–54A; P:I, 115; T:98; Z:69.

35–36. *In the year . . . and leisure. Essays,* ed. Villey, I, xxvii–xxviii, lxi–lxii; ed. Zeitlin, I, xxxiv; Plattard, *Montaigne et son temps,* p. 107 note. For the meaning here of "the Court," see Plattard, p. 86 note.

37. *One authority . . . all the humanists.* Léontine Zanta, *La Renaissance du stoïcisme au XVIe siècle* (Champion, 1914), p. 250.

37–38. *The soul that . . . ashamed of them.* I:8, 52–53A; P:I, 40; T:49; Z:23–24.

38. *he tells us . . . to a fine boy.* II:8, 141–42ABC; P:III, 102–3; T:384; Z:65.

38. *A stirred . . . to act on.* I:4, 35A; P:I, 24–25; T:40; Z:15.

38. *But the books . . . and my death.* I:39, 473A; P:II, 148; T:248; Z:217.

39. *Montaigne himself . . . little foreign.* III:5, 185C; P:V, 131; T:848; Z:84.

40. *The wretchedness . . . can hope for.* II:12, 319–20A; P:III, 233–34; T:474; Z:152. Cf. DB:II, 82–83. Cf. also I:14, 85A; P:I, 63; T:64; Z:38.

40. *Though he . . . of his friend.* I:28, 372A; P:II, 75–76; T:202; Z:171.

40. *My poor master! . . . good daughter!* III:4, 106B; P:V, 74–75; T:810; Z:45.

40–41. *In his gloomy . . . contempt, and disease.* I:39, 462–65A; P:II, 140–42; T: 243–44; Z:212–13.

41–42. *That is why . . . from my heart.* I:19, 143A; P:I, 107; T:93; Z:64.

42. *The deaths of Cato . . . with constancy.* II:13, 551A, 555A; P:IV, 12, 14; T:595, 597; Z:273, 275. Cf. DB:II, 189.

42. *probably . . . (in 1573 or 1574).* Montaigne's information is tantalizing. He tells us in this chapter that the event he narrates happened four years before, during the "second or third" civil war: that is, between 1567 and 1570. But he is likelier to be this vague about the third war than the second. Everything happens as though his father were dead and he lord of the manor, and his solicitude for his wife might well be caused by one of her pregnancies. All these things suggest the dates of 1569–70 for the event, 1573–74 for the chapter.

42–43. *Before he had . . . too much advantage.* II:6, 83A; P:III, 61; T:355; Z:37.

44–45. *In an early . . . has no remedy.* I:24, 249A; P:I, 184; T:144–45; Z:114–15.

45. *He knows . . . but even laudable.* I:14, 87–94A; P:I, 65–69; T:65–68; Z:39–42. I:23, 213A; P:I, 158; T:127; Z:98. I:39, 467A, 473A; P:II, 143–44, 148; T:245, 248; Z:214, 217.

45. *an aristocratic . . . were concerned.* Alan M. Boase, *The Fortunes of Montaigne: A History of the "Essays" in France, 1580–1669* (London: Methuen, 1935), p. xxxiv.

45. *the man of understanding.* I:39, 461A; P:II, 139; T:242; Z:211.

45. *It is he . . . thinking about death.* I:18, 134A; P:I, 101; T:88–89; Z:60–61. I:20, 155A; P:I, 116; T:98; Z:70.

45–46. *I cannot believe . . . effects of habit.* I:39, 468A; P:II, 144; T:246; Z:215.

46. *This is what . . . plan of nature . . . ?* I:14, 94A; P:I, 69–70; T:69; Z:42.

46. *Though something less . . . wares too dear.* I:20, 150A, 154–55A; P:I, 112, 115–16; T: 96, 98; Z:68, 70.

46. *Men are much . . . common herd?* I:14, 86A, 97–98A; P:I, 64, 72–73; T:64–65, 70–71; Z:38, 44.

47. *In "The Inconsistency of Our Actions" . . . from others.* II:1, 9–12A, 19A; P:III, 8–10, 16; T:319–21, 325; Z:1–3, 7.

47–48. *Matching his . . . Heaven and earth.* I:42, 495–500A and *passim;* P:II, 163–67; T:257–60; Z:226–29. Cf. DB:I, 217–18.

3: THE SKEPTICAL REVOLT

50. *According to . . . one or the other.* Jacques-Auguste de Thou, *Mémoires,* tr. Le Maserier *et al.,* in J. A. C. Buchon, *Panthéon littéraire: Choix de chroniques et mémoires sur l'histoire de France. XVIe siècle* (Desrez, 1836), pp. 628–29. See Strowski, *Montaigne, sa vie publique et privée,* pp. 174–75.

50. *Montaigne tells . . . 1572 or 1573.* I:14, 110–16B; P:I, 82–87; T:77–80; Z:50–53.

50. *I once tried . . . dangerous for that.* III:9, 415BC; P:VI, 74; T:962–63; Z:196.

51. *He was involved . . . over successions.* Nicolaï, "Montaigne homme privé et public," *Bulletin des Amis de Montaigne* (March 1, 1940), p. 8.

51. *He tells us . . . no details.* II:37, 850A; P:IV, 227; T:735; Z:409.

51. *Often in the . . . than his own.* See, for example, III:10, 471B; P:VI, 114; T:991; Z:223.

51. *He is a weak . . . and flabbiness.* F. J. Billeskov Jansen, *Les Sources vives de la pensée de Montaigne* (Copenhagen: Levin and Munksgaard, E. Munksgaard, 1935), pp. 56–57.

52. *Crawling on . . . heroic souls.* I:37, 441A; P:II, 124–25; T:233; Z:201. Cf. DB:I, 193.

52. *For intention . . . beyond our powers.* I:7, 49A; P:I, 36–37; T:47; Z:22.

52. *We know how . . . our own wisdom.* I:25, 259–61A; P:I, 191–93; T:149; Z:118–19. Cf. DB:I, 94.

52. *He sought harmony . . . not conflict.* II:11, 190A; P:III, 137; T:408; Z:87.

52. *It is by . . . and feel it.* II:3, 48A; P:III, 35–36; T:338; Z:20. Cf. DB:I, 289.

53. *whereas stoicism . . . vices as equal.* II:2, 22A; P:III, 17; T:325; Z:7.

53. *As proof that . . . for it not to.* I:21, 181–86A; P:I, 135–38; T:112–14; Z:84–86.

53. *I know by . . . confuses it.* I:10, 66A; P:I, 49–50; T:55; Z:29–30. Cf. DB:I, 25.

53–54. *More and more . . . at his action.* II:2, 36–37A; P:III, 28; T:333–34; Z:15. Cf. DB:I, 284. See also I:44, 519A; P:II, 181; T:268–69; Z:238. Also the passage (II:10, 163A; P:III, 118; T: 394; Z:74) where in 1578 Montaigne applies his phrase "undulating and diverse" to the tensely heroic Seneca.

54. *Posidonius was suffering . . . calling it an evil?* I:14, 94–95A; P:I, 70–71 (wrongly marked B); T:69; Z:43.

54. *The sage . . . impassible colossus.* I:44, 519A; P:II, 181; T:268; Z:238.

54. *Seneca's advice . . . Christian moderation.* I:33, 421A; P:II, 110–11; T:225; Z:193.

55. *Out of a thousand . . . is not in him.* II:2, 33–35A; P:III, 25–27; T:331–33; Z:13–14. Cf. DB:I, 282–83.

55. *He seems to sympathize with this view.* Otherwise he would hardly need to introduce it by a circumspect paragraph which clearly suggests that he knows that these ideas are not approved by the Church (II:3, 40–44A; P:III, 30–33; T:334–36; Z:16–18). Even later, in his *Travel Journal,* he regards suicide as a legitimate alternative to intolerable pain (p. 384; La Villa, Aug. 24, 1581; see below, p. 119).

56. *The opinion that . . . and combat oneself.* II:3, 47–48A; P:III, 35; T:338; Z:20. Cf. DB:I, 289.

56. *As if our touch . . . and by study.* I:30, 378–79A, 384A; P:II, 81, 85; T:205–6, 208; Z:174, 176–77. Cf. DB: I, 163.

57. *Socrates . . . only three times.* I:14, 87A; P:I, 65; T:65; Z:39. I:39, 459A; P:II, 137; T:241; Z:210. II:2, 34A; P:III, 26; T:332; Z:13–14. Another reference in an early essay (I:23, 221A; P:I, 164; T:131; Z:102) is an addition of 1582 (see DB:I, 79*n*). I am relying here on Villey's dating and on the Index of Proper Names in his edition.

58. *Perfidy . . . hated and scorned.* II:18, 669–70A; P:IV, 97 (wrongly marked B); T:652–53; Z:328.

58. *Most of the . . . Margaret of Valois.* See D. M. Frame, "Did Montaigne Betray Sebond?" *Romanic Review,* XXXVIII (December, 1947), 297–329.

60. *Montaigne was a skeptic . . . seems excessive.* His fideism, his skepticism, and his notion of flux are fully and clearly in his mind

in such chapters as I:23 ("Of Custom and of Not Easily Changing an Accepted Law"), I:27 ("It Is Folly to Measure the True and False by Our Own Capacity"), I:32 ("We Must Meddle Soberly with Judging Divine Ordinances"), and I:47 ("Of the Uncertainty of Our Judgment"), as well as in his latest—III:8 ("Of the Art of Conversing"), III:13 ("Of Experience"), and others.

60–61. *Montaigne's account . . . we believe in.* II:12, 340A; P:III, 249–50; T:485; Z:163.

61. *I often risk . . . that I mistrust.* III:8, 319B; P:V, 228–29; T:915; Z:149.

61. *For example . . . what is true.* II:12, 453–56A; P:III, 337–40; T:545–47; Z:223–25.

61. *they demonstrate . . . (vraisemblables) things.* II:12, 477A; P:III, 354; T:557–58; Z:235. Cf. DB:II, 154.

61–62. *As for the actions . . . and gave up.* II:12, 344–45A; P:III, 252–53; T:487–88; Z:165. Cf. DB:II, 95.

62. *man without divine grace or knowledge.* II:12, 234A; P:III, 168; T:429; Z:107. These are not Montaigne's exact words, which read as follows: ". . . man alone . . . unprovided with divine grace and knowledge. . . ."

62. *Presumption is . . . of other creatures.* II:12, 239A; P:III, 172; T:432; Z:110. Cf. DB:II, 32.

62–63. *To crush and . . . divine majesty.* II:12, 232A; P:III, 166; T:428; Z:106.

63. *We are all . . . needs to be content.* II:12, 277A, 284A; P:III, 201, 206; T:452, 455; Z:130, 133–34.

63–64. *Even if we do . . . rejoice in it . . . ?* II:12, 304–14A; P:III, 221–29; T:466–71; Z:144–49. Cf. DB:II, 79.

64–65. *Here is Posidonius . . . to forget it.* II:12, 314–23A; P:III, 229–36; T:471–76; Z:149–54. Cf. DB:II, 79–80.

65. *Even suicide . . . obedience and submission.* II:12, 309–11A, 326–34A; P:III, 225–26, 238–45; T:468–69, 477–82; Z:146–47, 155–60. Cf. DB:II, 89.

66. *Yet must I . . . any solid truth.* II:12, 334A; P:III, 245; T:482; Z:160.

66. *I wish to take . . . as its own.* II:12, 337A; P:III, 247–48; T:483–84; Z:161. Cf. DB:II, 91.

66. *Among them is Socrates . . . ever was.* II:12, 335A; P:III, 246; T:483; Z:160.

67. *It presents man . . . thy knowledge.* II:12, 346–47A; P:III, 254–55; T:488–89; Z:166. Important corrections from DB:II, 95–96.

67. *Most of the dogmatists . . . theorizing anyway.* II:12, 347–55A; P:III, 255–61; T:489–93; Z:166–70. Cf. DB:II, 97.

67–68. *It is impossible . . . it might be.* II:12, 356–60A; P:III, 262–65; T:494–96; Z:171–73. Cf. DB:II, 100.

68. *Here, indeed, as elsewhere . . . human opinions.* II:12, 374–90A; P:III, 275–87; T:503–12; Z:180–89.

68. *In our knowledge . . . for themselves.* II:12, 404–16A; P:III, 299–308; T:520–26; Z:197–203.

68. *Reason, they tell . . . knows nothing.* II:12, 416–47A; P:III, 308–32; T:526–43; Z:203–20.

68–69. *Montaigne now . . . intrinsically impotent.* II:12, 447–51A; P:III, 333–36; T:543–45; Z:221–22.

69. *Some say that . . . a distortion.* II:12, 451–57A; P:III, 336–41; T:545–48; Z:222–26.

69. *We can see . . . does not know.* II:12, 459–72A; P:III, 341–51; T:548–55; Z:226–32.

69–70. *Change is the . . . ideas of ours.* II:12, 473–501A; P:III, 352–72; T:555–69; Z:233–47.

70. *Our senses are . . . by his virtue.* II:12, 510–21AB; P:III, 378–87; T:574–80; Z:251–57.

70–71. *Probably deficient . . . two are alike.* II:12, 527–38A; P:III, 391–99; T:583–89; Z:260–67.

71. *Finally . . . above humanity!* II:12, 538–44A; P:III, 399–403; T:589–92; Z:267–69.

71. *There is no truer . . . but not otherwise.* See variants, listed in notes, on II:12, 544; P:III, 403; T:592; Z:269. DB:II, 186.

73. *That is a good . . . miraculous metamorphosis.* II:12, 544C; P:III, 403; T:592; Z:269.

4: SELF-DISCOVERY AND LIBERATION

74. *Twice Condé . . . for the Reformists.* See Dreano, *Pensée religieuse de Montaigne,* pp. 153–54.

75. *He seems to . . . have no details.* II:37, 850A; P:IV, 227; T:735; Z:409. Cf. Beuther's *Ephemeris,* Nov. 29, 1577.

75. *Villey suspects . . . different strata.* Villey, *Les Sources et l'évolution,* II, 171–72.

75. *Zeitlin develops . . . and attitude.* Z:II, 494–95.

76. *For every . . . between them.* II:12, 414A; P:III, 306–7; T:525; Z:202.

77. *Even without God's . . . our follies.* II:12, 459A; P:III, 342; T:549; Z:226.

77. *He never quite . . . to know it.* Already the elements of this attitude are all present; later he will virtually admit it (see below, p. 158).

77–78. *The appalling . . . and cruelty.* II:12, 217–26A; P:III, 154–61; T:420–25; Z:98–103.

78. *Since nothing created . . . come back home.* Montaigne, *Œuvres complètes,* IX, 2.

78–79. *Montaigne says . . . settle in itself.* I:8, 52A; P:I, 40; T:49; Z:23.

79. *For independence . . . making ready.* I:39, *passim.*

79. *The worst he . . . for ourselves.* I:25, 259–64A; P:I, 191–94; T:149–51; Z:118–20.

79. *This account of . . . it is mine.* II:6, 93A; P:III, 69; T:360; Z:42.

79. *The know-it-alls . . . knowing themselves.* II:12, 410A; P:III, 303; T:523; Z:200.

79. *If man knew . . . and easiest.* II:12, 447A; P:III, 332; T:542–43; Z:220.

79. *I who watch . . . find in myself.* II:12, 464A; P:III, 345; T:551; Z:229.

79. *He does not . . . the same lesson.* II:12, 466B; P:III, 346; T:552; Z:230.

79. *each man can . . . as he pleases.* II:12, 520A; P:III, 386; T:579; Z:256–57.

80. *Since philosophy . . . individually!* II:16, 580C; P:IV, 33; T:608–9; Z:286.

80. *What reveals man . . . the everyday.* See especially II:1, *passim.* I:50, 578A; P:II, 224; T:295; Z:265.

80. *Judgment is . . . how to live.* See especially I:23, 218A; P:I, 162; T:130; Z:100. I:25, 266–71A; P:I, 196–200; T:152–55; Z:121–24.

I:26, 289A and *passim;* P:II, 16; T:163; Z:132. I:50, 577A; P:II, 223; T:295; Z:265. II:8, 111A; P:III, 80; T:368; Z:50. II:10, 154–58A; P:III, 111–14; T:390–92; Z:70–71. II:11, 193A; P:III, 139; T:410; Z:88. II:12, 459–64A; P:III, 341–45; T:548–51; Z:226–29. II:17, 599–600A, 649–53A; P:IV, 47, 82–85; T:618, 643–45; Z:295, 319–21.

80–81. *I take no stock . . . and my work.* II:37, 902A; P:IV, 264; T:762; Z:433.

81. *He is weary . . . understand themselves.* II:17, 605A; P:IV, 51; T:620–21; Z:298. I:25, 263–64A; P:I, 194; T:151; Z:120.

81. *The popular Renaissance . . . Aristotle's observations.* II:12, 407–13A; P:III, 300–305; T:522–24; Z:198–201. Cf. III:5, 182B; P:V, 130; T:847; Z:83.

81. *Each bit . . . us in motion.* II:1, 18–20A; P:III, 15–16; T:324–25; Z:67. Cf. DB:I, 278.

81. *There is no . . . man to himself.* II:16, 587A; P:IV, 38; T:612; Z:290. Cf. DB:II, 206.

81–82. *Now these opinions . . . principally to myself.* II:17, 652A; P:IV, 84–85; T:644; Z:321. Cf. DB:II, 236–37.

82–83. *Judgment is a . . . to make us known.* I:50, 577–78A; P:II, 223–24; T:295; Z:265. Cf. DB:I, 252. This is the account, mentioned above, that cannot be dated surely.

83. *Madam . . . unnatural plan.* II:8, 108A; P:III, 78; T:366–67; Z:48–49.

83–84. *His main task . . . step as it is.* I:26, 282A; P:II, 11; T:159; Z:128. II:10, 152–57A; P:III, 110–13; T:388–91; Z:69–71. Cf. DB:I, 340.

84. *His language . . . I like it that way.* II:17, 612A; P:IV, 56; T:624; Z:301–2. Cf. DB:II, 218.

84. *In order to be . . . he will reveal.* I:26, 282A; P:II, 11; T:159; Z:128. II:37, 850A; P:IV, 227; T:735; Z:409.

84. *Whatever these . . . face, but mine.* I:26, 282A; P:II, 11; T:159; Z:128.

84. *Even if I had . . . have done it.* II:37, 901A; P:IV, 263; T:761; Z:433.

84. *I want to be . . . that I portray.* I: To the Reader, 4A; P:I, 2; T:25; Z:1. Cf. DB:I, 2.

85. *I see well . . . them as such.* II:17, 643A; P:IV, 78; T:639–40; Z:316–17.

86. *Our conception . . . from the object.* II:12, 537–38A; P:III, 398–99; T:588–89; Z:266.

86. *It is in the . . . by a compromise.* "If the original being of these things that we fear had the power of lodging in us by its own authority, it would lodge the same and alike in us all; for men are all of a kind. . . . But the diversity of the opinions that we have of those things shows clearly that they enter us only by compromise; a given man perhaps lodges them in himself in their own true being, but a thousand others give them a new and contrary being within them" (I:14, 86A; P:I, 64; T:64–65; Z:38).

86–87. *But this advice . . . accomplish very much.* I:14, 97–101A, 120A; P:I, 72–75, 89; T:70–72, 82; Z:44–46, 54–55.

87. *The privilege . . . to the beasts.* II:12, 297A; P:III, 216; T:462; Z:140.

87. *That things . . . as we please.* II:12, 457A; P:III, 340; T:548; Z:225. Cf. DB:II, 142.

87. *For cognition is . . . their own essence.* II:12, 510A; P:III, 378; T:574; Z:251.

87–88. *The senses are . . . and lies.* II:12, 527–28A; P:III, 391–92; T:583–84; Z:260–61. Cf. DB:II, 176–77.

88. *The main responsibility . . . appearance as sickness?* II:12, 535A; P:III, 397; T:587–88; Z:265. Cf. DB:II, 180.

88. *He finds our taste . . . but altered.* II:20, 681A; P:IV, 105; T:657; Z:333.

88. *He shows . . . a good husband.* II:17, 615A; P:IV, 58; T:625–26; Z:303.

88. *When, as we shall see . . . of the pain.* II:37, 852–57A; P:IV, 229–32; T:736–39; Z:410–12.

88–89. *The soul, he finds . . . ourselves alone.* I:14, 99–100C; P:I, 74; T:72; Z:45. I:50, 579C; P:II, 224–25; T:296; Z:265–66. For these passages in full, see below, pp. 144–46.

89. *But now he . . . equally unhappy.* II:15, 559–63A; P:IV, 18–21; T:599–601; Z:277–79.

90. *I find in him . . . I need air.* Michelet, *Histoire de France* (Chamerot, 1856 ed.), X, 400–401.

91. *There are only . . . blocked by it.* II:3, 51A; P:III, 38; T:340; Z:22. Cf. DB:I, 291.

91. *He wrote in 1572 . . . pain thus far.* I:14, 97A; P:I, 72; T:70; Z:44.

91. *A year or two . . . truth of the thing.* II:6, 82–83A; P:III, 61; T:355; Z:37.

92. *The stone . . . terrible pain.* II:37, 850A, 860A; P:IV, 228, 234; T:735, 740; Z:409, 413–14.

92. *The fear of . . . not bear it.* III:13, 615B; P:VI, 217; T:1061; Z:291.

92. *It had even . . . vain propositions.* II:37, 851A; P:IV, 228; T:735–36; Z:409.

92–94. *I was so far . . . of their reasoning.* II:37, 851–59A; P:IV, 228–33; T:736–40; Z:409–13. Cf. DB:II, 327–31.

95. *The soul in which . . . teaches us to live.* I:26, 308A, 312A; P:II, 30, 32–33; T:172–74; Z:141, 143. Cf. DB:I, 115.

5: THE FREE MAN

96. *Mr. Hiram Haydn . . . finds is Montaigne.* See *The Counter-Renaissance* (New York: Scribner's, 1950), pp. 468–97.

97. *When I encounter . . . other creatures.* II:11, 204–5A; P:III, 147–49; T:416; Z:94–95. Cf. DB:II, 16.

97. *Obviously they . . . World for the New.* La Boétie's Latin poem to Montaigne and Belot, which expresses this wish, is usually dated earlier than Montaigne's talk with the cannibals. But it sounds much as though his country were at war; and if so, it may have been written later.

98–99. *They are wild . . . pardon, unheard of.* I:31, 395–98A; P:II, 92–94; T:213–14; Z:181–83. Cf. DB:I, 170–71. Cf. *The Tempest* II.i.154–75.

Another civilized occupation that Montaigne could have done without, and in his time a form of humanism at that, was medicine (II:37, 861–96A; P:IV, 235–59; T:741–59; Z:414–31; etc.).

99. *We are pleased . . . content with it.* I:31, 404–6A; P:II, 98–100; T:217–18; Z:185–86. III:13, 666B; P:VI, 255; T:1088; Z:316.

99. *It is not . . . don't wear breeches.* I:31, 412–14A; P:II, 104–6; T:221–22; Z:189–90.

100. *Since it has . . . our inclinations.* II:8, 111A; P:III, 80; T:368; Z:50. Cf. DB:I, 319.

100–101. *In a chapter . . . cannot endure them.* I:54, 596–97A and *passim;* P:II, 239; T:304; Z:274.

101. *Curiously, Socrates . . . good as Socrates.* II:36, 846A and *passim;* P:IV, 224; T:733; Z:407 (wrongly marked C).

102. *Montaigne's new . . . in "Cruelty" (II:11).* In other essays of this period the three levels appear. In "Cannibals" (I:31) Montaigne praises witnesses who are either simple or both clever and honest. The merely clever ones, he finds, alter facts to fit their theories. In "Books" (II:10) he pays tribute to the simple and the very judicious historians, while condemning those who try to judge but cannot.

102–3. *Virtue, he begins . . . superior to innocence.* II:11, 179–88A; P:III, 129–35; T:403–7; Z:81–85. Cf. DB:II, 2, 4.

103. *Furthermore, Montaigne . . . as I could.* II:11, 190–93A; P:III, 137–39; T:408–10; Z:86–88.

104. *and that La Boëtie . . . gifts by study.* II:17, 656A; P:IV, 87; T:646; Z:322.

104. *Of all the . . . of ourselves.* II:17, 604–5A; P:IV, 51; T:620; Z:298. Cf. DB:II, 214.

104–5. *By now he . . . of our defects.* I:18. I:21. I:23. I:26, 284A; P:II, 12; T:160; Z:129. II:1. II:2, 33–35A; P:III, 25–27; T:331–33; Z:13–14. II:4, 69A; P:III, 51; T:349; Z:31. II:5. II:12.

105. *Our inability . . . a bad education.* I:25, 265A; P:I, 195–96; T:151; Z:121.

105. *Custom and habit . . . type of virtue.* I:23, 200A, 205A, 213A; P:I, 149, 152–53, 158; T:121, 123, 127; Z:92, 94, 98. II:11, 187A; P:III, 135; T:407; Z:85.

105–6. *The conscience . . . gratifying of rewards.* II:16, 582A; P:IV, 35; T:610; Z:288.

106. *The body has . . . and uniform.* II:17, 615A; P:IV, 58; T:625–26; Z:303. Cf. DB:II, 220.

106. *In one of . . . a thing to fear.* I:39, 468A; P:II, 144; T:245–46; Z:215. See above, p. 41.

107. *I welcome health . . . mind brings us.* II:12, 317A; P:III, 231; T:472; Z:150. Cf. DB:II, 81.

107–8. *I am at grips . . . of their reasoning.* II:37, 853A, 858–59A; P:IV, 229, 233; T:737, 740; Z:410, 413.

108. *Nobler beings . . . peculiar to man.* II:3, 47–48A; P:III, 35; T:338; Z:20. See above, p. 56.

108. *Even the elements . . . distinctive quality.* II:17, 605–6A, 649A, 652A; P:IV, 51, 82–85; T:620–21, 643–44; Z:298, 319–21.

108. *He is always . . . communication.* I:26, 319A and *passim;* P:II, 38; T:177; Z:146.

109. *The greatest thing . . . to oneself.* I:39, 465A; P:II, 142; T:244; Z:213.

109. *I do not . . . diversity and discord.* II:37, 906A; P:IV, 266–67; T:764; Z:435. Cf. DB:II, 364.

6: THE DISCOVERY OF OTHERS

110. *Thus, reader . . . March, 1580.* I: To the Reader, 4A; P:I, 2; T:25; Z:1. Cf. DB:I, 2.

111. *It has been . . . ambassador to Venice.* See Charles Dédéyan, *Essai sur le "Journal de Voyage" de Montaigne* (Boivin, n. d.), pp. 30, 98–105, and Maurice Rat's review of Nicolaï (*Les Belles Amies*) in *Figaro Littéraire,* December 16, 1950, p. 7.

111. *he desired less . . . to every man. JV:*164; Rovereto, Oct. 29, 1580.

111–12. *More important . . . from his wife.* I:39, 458A; P:II, 137; T:241; Z:209. III:9, *passim.*

112. *The condition of . . . other considerations. JV:*124; Lindau, Oct. 10, 1580.

112. *I know well . . . an uncertain one.* III:9, 376–77B; P:VI, 45–46; T:942; Z:176.

112–13. *A final motive . . . for other things.* I:26, 291A, 300–302A; P:II, 18, 24–25; T:163–64, 168–69; Z:133, 137–38. Cf. DB:I, 111.

113. *Thus after . . . public visage. JV:*241; Rome, March 29–31, 1581.

113. *Wherever he went . . . various cities. JV:*188–89, 193; Florence, Nov. 22–24, 1580.

113. *From all the . . . comfort-loving people. JV:*102–5; Basel, Sept. 29–Oct. 1, 1580.

113–14. *Around the beds . . . use them for. JV:*149; Innsbruck, Oct. 23, 1580. The secretary may be responsible for the degree of emphasis on details of living in the parts that he wrote down; but Montaigne's lively interest in these matters is unquestionable.

114. *Monsieur de Montaigne . . . for a napkin.* *JV*:111; Baden, Oct. 2–7, 1580.

114. *A few days . . . wine without water.* *JV*:124–25; Lindau, Oct. 10, 1580.

114. *The first . . . humor of the nation.* *JV*:97; Plombières, Sept. 27, 1580.

114. *In Augsburg . . . around the town.* *JV*:138; Augsburg, Oct. 15–19, 1580.

115. *Monsieur de Montaigne . . . Catholics there.* *JV*:99; Mulhousen, Sept. 29, 1580.

115. *In Rome . . . cosmopolitan town.* *JV*:210, 243; Rome, January and March–April, 1581.

115. *There, too, he . . . France again.* *JV*:290–444; La Villa–Lanslebourg, May 13–Nov. 1, 1581.

115. *Even though . . . to do so.* III:5, 180B; P:V, 128; T:846; Z:82.

115. *He is irritated . . . countries he visits.* *JV*:156; Brixen, Oct. 26, 1580.

115. *They are a . . . conform to them.* *JV*:111; Baden, Oct. 2–7, 1580.

115. *The people around . . . law-abiding.* *JV*:94; Plombières, Sept. 16–27, 1580.

115. *From Bolzano . . . has found there.* *JV*:159; Bolzano, Oct. 27, 1580.

115–16. *He finds the Roman . . . the city offers.* *JV*:218, 240–42; Rome, February and March–April, 1581.

116. *Even what . . . a good friend.* *JV*:344; Florence, June 26, 1581. *JV*:370–73; Lucca, July 28, 1581. Only once does he complain of his treatment (*JV*:430; Fornovo, Oct. 23, 1581).

116. *Whether or not . . . Roman citizenship.* *JV*:203–4, 243; Rome, Dec. 29, 1580, and April 5, 1581.

116. *Montaigne is readily . . . ambassador is not.* *JV*:222–24; Rome, March 6, 1581.

116. *The distinguished . . . seeks him out.* *JV*:239–40; Rome, March 29, 1581. Cf. *JV*:85–86; Epernay, Sept. 8, 1580.

116. *One tribute . . . here and in Rome.* *JV*:322–23; La Villa, May 31, 1581.

116. *There were great . . . come back home. JV*:376–77; La Villa, Aug. 13, 1581.

117–18. *On Whitsunday . . . delightful time. JV*:294–95, 300–309; La Villa, May 14 and 21, 1581.

118. *He compares . . . himself to consider. JV*:163–64; Rovereto, Oct. 29, 1580.

118. *The valley of . . . has ever seen. JV*:148; Mittenwald–Innsbruck, Oct. 23, 1580.

118. *Even extreme . . . of that place. JV*:252; Narni–Foligno, April 21, 1581.

118. *Altogether the . . . diverted his trouble. JV*:164; Rovereto, Oct. 29, 1580.

118. *Sainte-Beuve to . . . ever lived. Nouveaux Lundis* (M. and C. Lévy, 1870–83 eds.), II, 177; cf. pp. 156–76.

119. *Finally on . . . and promptly. JV*:382–85; La Villa, Aug. 24, 1581.

119–20. *These are perhaps . . . his thought.* The best treatment of these matters is in Imbrie Buffum's excellent *L'Influence du voyage de Montaigne sur les "Essais"* (Princeton, New Jersey, 1946).

120. *Generally he . . . only for his friends.* See for example II:18, 664–65A; P:IV, 93–94; T:649–50; Z:325–26.

120. *The favor of . . . in good part.* III:9, 361–62B; P:VI, 35; T:935; Z:169.

120. *Later he . . . they buy him.* III:2, 48C; P:V, 34; T:783; Z:18–19.

120. *Henry III must . . . life and actions.* This story is told by La Croix du Maine. See below, pp. 122–23.

120–22. *When Montaigne first . . . be well satisfied. JV*:201, 232–33, 247–48; Rome, Nov. 30, 1580, March 20 and April 15, 1581. The Master of the Sacred Palace at this time was Sisto Fabri of Lucca (1541–94), professor of theology at the University of Rome, and soon (1583) to be general of the Dominican order. His "learned monks" were also Dominicans. The passages criticized in the *Essays,* in order of mention, are the following or others like them: II:4, 69A; P:III, 51; T:349; Z:31. II:17, 659A; P:IV, 90; T:648; Z:324. II:19. I:56. II:11 and I:27. I:26, 320A; P:II, 38; T:177; Z:146–47. For two comments by Montaigne, who made no use of the criticisms, see I:56, 618BC; P:II, 252–53; T:313; Z:283. III:10, 457C; P:VI, 103; T:983; Z:216.

122. *By 1584 . . . is now known.* See La Croix du Maine, *Bibliothèque françoise,* s.v. "Michel de Montagne."

122–24. *The Essays were . . . soon to follow.* See especially the *Bibliothèques françoises* of La Croix du Maine and Antoine du Verdier, s.v. "Michel de Montagne." Essential texts and sound discussion of all these early readers of Montaigne are found in Villey, *Montaigne devant la postérité* (Boivin, 1935), pp. 20–28, 343–48.

124–25. *New light shed . . . ambassador to Venice.* For the events leading up to Montaigne's mayoralty, see Nicolaï, *Les Belles Amies,* pp. 135–45. For the Venetian ambassadorship, see Maurice Rat's review of *Les Belles Amies,* in *Figaro Littéraire,* December 16, 1950, p. 7.

125. *He first heard . . . ever endured. JV*:392–93; La Villa, Sept. 7, 1581.

125. *found his official . . . the jurats. JV*:414–15, Rome, Oct. 1, 1581.

125–26. *Monsieur de Montaigne . . . displease me.* Quoted in Bonnefon, *Montaigne,* p. 305; Nicolaï, *Les Belles Amies,* pp. 143–44.

126. *Montaigne's confidence . . . his own ulcers.* III:10, 441–43B; P:VI, 92–93; T:975–76; Z:208–9.

126–29. *His first two-year . . . his Essays.* Good accounts of this period in Montaigne's life are in Strowski, *Montaigne, sa vie publique et privée,* pp. 203–21; Bonnefon, *Montaigne,* pp. 307–411. The best original sources are Montaigne's "Of Husbanding Your Will" (III:10) and "Of Physiognomy" (III:12), his notes on Beuther's *Ephemeris,* and his letters (*Œuvres complètes,* Vol. XI). For Margaret of Valois, see Nicolaï, *Les Belles Amies,* pp. 145–70. For Duplessis-Mornay, see his *Mémoires et correspondance* (12 vols.; Treuttel et Wurtz, 1824–25), II, 382–402, 518–19. For Corisande d'Andoins de Gramont, see Raymond Ritter, *Cette Grande Corisande* (Michel, 1936), pp. 188–206, 212; Nicolaï, *Les Belles Amies;* and Montaigne, *Œuvres complètes,* XI, 233–34. On the armed review, see *Essays* I:24, 246–47B; P:I, 182–83 (wrongly marked A); T:143; Z:113. On the siege of Castillon and Montaigne's flight with his family from the plague, see Roger Trinquet, "Du nouveau dans la biographie de Montaigne," *Revue d'Histoire Littéraire de la France* (January–March 1953), pp. 5–16.

129. *I did not leave . . . my own action.* III:10, 474–80B; P:VI, 116–20; T:992–95; Z:224–27.

130. *The Remonstrance . . . costs of the wars.* Montaigne, *Œuvres complètes,* XI, 215–25.

130. *His natural languor . . . well guided.* III:10, 473–74B; P:VI, 115–16; T:991–92; Z:224.

130. *Nor did he . . . the humble more.* See, for example, III:7 ("Of the Disadvantage of Greatness").

131. *His father . . . worked pretty well.* III:13, 634–35B; P:VI, 231–32; T:1070–71; Z:300–301.

131. *that is not . . . faculties idle.* II:12, 337A; P:III, 247; T:483; Z:161.

131–32. *In the ten . . . for religion.* II:32, 781–82A; P:IV, 178–79; T:703; Z:377–78.

132. *it is not so new . . . virtue rarely lodge.* II:35, 823–24A; P:IV, 208–9; T:723; Z:397.

132. *The souls of . . . we are in ours.* An addition of 1582. II:12, 286A; P:III, 207–8; T:456; Z:134. Cf. DB:II, 61.

132. *We are so in love . . . only to die.* III:12, 506–7B, 513–14B; P:VI, 138, 143–44; T:1006, 1010; Z:238, 241–42.

132. *When the heaviest . . . and he with them.* III:12, 520B; P:VI, 148; T:1013; Z:245.

133. *Now what . . . deliberated resoluteness.* III:12, 529–31B; P:VI, 155–57; T:1018–19; Z:250–51.

133. *It is certain . . . school of stupidity.* III:12, 534–38B; P:VI, 159–62; T:1020–22; Z:252–54.

133–34. *An element . . . but it is small.* III:12, 512–13B and *passim;* P:VI, 143; T:1009–10; Z:241.

134. *And in truth . . . even to the wicked.* III:12, 554–55B, 559–60B; P:VI, 174, 177–78; T:1031, 1033–34; Z:261, 264.

134. *He is convinced . . . specimen of mankind.* III:2, 40B; P:V, 29; T:779; Z:15. See below, p. 142.

134. *now he finds . . . somewhat for others.* III:10, 444–45BC; P:VI, 94–95; T:976–77; Z:210.

7: THE WHOLE MAN

136. *We have no record . . . than rebellion.* See Strowski, *Montaigne, sa vie publique et privée,* pp. 234–43; Ritter, *Cette Grande Corisande,* pp. 188–206, 246–55.

136–37. *Three and a half . . . His Majesty wishes.* See Ritter, *Cette Grande Corisande,* pp. 254–55; Strowski, *Montaigne, sa vie publique et privée,* pp. 243–44; Nicolaï, *Les Belles Amies,* pp. 42–43, 178–79. Presumably "what His Majesty wishes" is for Navarre to abjure his Protestantism.

137. *The League was . . . of his arrest.* See Beuther's *Ephemeris,* in *Œuvres complètes,* XI, 283–85.

137. *Montaigne was very . . . with him there.* See Strowski, *Montaigne, sa vie publique et privée,* pp. 247–52; Nicolaï, *Les Belles Amies,* pp. 171–220.

138–39. *He tells Henry . . . of your officers.* Montaigne, *Œuvres complètes,* XI, 259–62, 264–65. The quotation "head high, face and heart open" is from *Essays* III:1, 14B; P:V, 11; T:767; Z:3.

139. *always be booted and ready to go.* I:20, 159A; P:I, 119; T:101; Z:72.

139. *It was a throat . . . Mass in his bed.* No eyewitness accounts exist. The main authorities are letters of Brach to Antony Bacon (see *Bulletin des Amis de Montaigne,* June 1, 1937) and of Etienne Pasquier to M. de Pelgé (Pasquier, *Œuvres choisies,* ed. Feugère [Didot, 1849], II, 396–97). See Strowski, *Montaigne, sa vie publique et privée,* pp. 265–66.

140. *Montaigne continues . . . in expression.* III:2, 55–64BC; P:V, 39–45; T:787–91; Z:22–26. III:12, 552C; P:VI, 172; T:1030; Z:260.

140. *More and more . . . knew his own.* III:2, 41B; P:V, 29; T:780; Z:15. III:11, 490–91B; P:VI, 127–28; T:999; Z:231.

140. *The essays become . . . movement of it.* III:9, 421–24B; P:VI, 78–80; T:965–67; Z:199–200.

142. *Natural inclinations . . . that oppose it.* III:2, 51–52B; P:V, 36–37; T:785; Z:20–21.

142. *Montaigne still . . . from the animals.* III:13, 563B, 572–73C; P:VI, 179–80, 186–87; T:1034, 1039; Z:265, 270.

142. *He finds that . . . conduct to them.* III:13, 585–86B; P:VI, 196; T:1046; Z:276.

142. *I set forth . . . man's estate.* III:2, 40B; P:V, 29; T:779; Z:15.

142–43. *the people of the New World . . . and women.* New World—III:6, 254–57B and *passim;* P:V, 182–84; T:883–84; Z:118–20. Foreigners—III:9, 378B, 404–5B; P:VI, 46–47, 65–66; T:943, 956–57; Z:177, 190. Bordeaux—III:10, 473–74B; P:VI, 115; T:992; Z:224.

Freaks—II:30, 759C; P:IV, 161–62; T:692–93; Z:367. Women—III:5, 228B; P:V, 163; T:870; Z:106.

143. *Christian doctrine . . . in this vein.* II:17, 615A; P:IV, 58; T:626; Z:303. III:13, 663–64BC; P:VI, 253; T:1086; Z:315.

143. *It is not a soul . . . be separated.* I:26, 316A; P:II, 36; T:176; Z:145.

143. *He had rejected . . . of our being.* II:12, 372–73A; P:III, 274; T:502–3; Z:179–80. Cf. DB:II, 105.

143. *Now he writes . . . a living man.* III:5, 219B; P:V, 156; T:866; Z:101.

143. *To what purpose . . . correspondence?* III:13, 663B; P:VI, 252; T:1086; Z:315.

143. *Again and again . . . and irregular.* III:9, 410B; P:VI, 70; T:959–60; Z:193. Cf. III:8, 293–94B; P:V, 210; T:902; Z:136.

143. *For the same . . . half of it.* III:5, 211C; P:V, 150; T:861–62; Z:97.

143–44. *The body as Montaigne . . . it stability.* III:2, 61B; P:V, 43–44; T:790; Z:25. III:10, 445–46B; P:VI, 95; T:977; Z:210–11. III: 13, 650B, 663B; P:VI, 243, 252; T:1079, 1086; Z:308, 315.

144. *The soul is . . . us miserable.* III:4, 110–12BC; P:V, 77–79; T:812–13; Z:47–48. III:12, 531B; P:VI, 156–57; T:1019; Z:251. III: 13, 648C; P:VI, 241; T:1077–78; Z:307.

144. *Its parts or . . . good or evil.* See especially III:2, 55B; P:V, 39; T:787; Z:22. III:13, 582B, 613–14B, 630B; P:VI, 193–94, 216, 228; T:1044, 1060, 1068; Z:275, 291, 298.

144–45. *Things in themselves . . . ourselves alone.* I:50, 579C; P:II, 224–25; T:296; Z:265–66.

145. *Since the soul is so . . . had seen earlier.* I:26, 308A; P:II, 30; T:172; Z:141. II:17, 615A; P:IV, 58; T:625–26; Z:303. See above, pp. 95, 106.

145. *In particular . . . well off indeed.* III:2, 61B, 65B; P:V, 43, 46; T:790–91; Z:25, 27. III:5, 115–20B; P:V, 80–84; T:813–16; Z:48–52. III:13, 630B; P:VI, 228; T:1068–69; Z:298–99.

145–46. *The body has . . . and contentment.* I:14, 99–100C; P:I, 74; T:72; Z:45.

146. *All this, of course . . . in importance.* See I:21, 186–88C; P:I, 139–40; T:115–16; Z:86–87. II:12, 232–34A and *passim;* P:III, 166–68; T:428–29; Z:106–7.

146. *Moreover, vice . . . of our life.* I:23, 203C; P:I, 151; T:122; Z:93. II:30, 759C; P:IV, 161–62; T:692–93; Z:367. III:1, 10–11B; P:V, 8–9; T:765–66; Z:1–2.

146. *However, we . . . and control it.* III:13, 580–81BC; P:VI, 192–93; T:1043–44; Z:273–74.

146. *To know it . . . night the day.* III:2, 43BC; P:V, 30–31; T:781; Z:16.

146. *I do not . . . as of inanity.* I:50, 581A; P:II, 226; T:297; Z:267. Cf. DB:I, 253.

146–47. *It is man's wisdom . . . belong to it.* III:3, 78B; P:V, 55; T:797; Z:32. III:4, 111B; P:V, 78; T:812; Z:48. Cf. III:4, 104–5B; P:V, 73–74; T:809–10; Z:44–45. III:5, 148B, 188–89BC, 209C; P:V, 105, 133–34, 149; T:830–31, 850, 861; Z:66, 86, 96. III:10, 437–55BC; P:VI, 89–102; T:973–82; Z:206–15. III:11, 485–87BC; P:VI, 123–25; T:996–98; Z:228–30. III:12, 505–13BC, 531–38BC; P:VI, 138–43, 156–62; T:1006–10, 1019–23; Z:238–41, 250–54. III:13, 648C; P:VI, 241; T:1078; Z:307.

147. *Vanity is the heart . . . fool of the farce.* III:9, 409BC, 433–34B; P:VI, 69–70, 87–88; T:959, 972–73; Z:193, 205–6. For the theme of vanity in still other essays of Book Three, see among others III:7, *passim* (vanity of the supposed pleasures of high station); III:8, 300–303BC; P:V, 215–17; T:905–7; Z:140–41 (vanity of our efforts to control fortune).

147. *Our essence, then . . . to the attack.* III:9, 409–14BC; P:VI, 69–73; T:959–62; Z:193–95. Cf. II:3, 47–48A; P:III, 35; T:338; Z:20.

148. *But at the same time . . . all we most need.* III:12, 509–10B, 531B, 552C; P:VI, 140–41, 156–57, 172; T:1008, 1019, 1030; Z:239–40, 251, 260–61. III:13, 580–81BC; P:VI, 191–93; T:1042–44; Z:272–74.

149. *The essence of . . . only the good.* I:26, 320A and *passim;* P:II, 38; T:177; Z:146–47. I:25, 261AB and *passim;* P:I, 192–93; T:149; Z:119.

149. *For Montaigne this . . . of integrity.* See III:2, 55B; P:V, 39; T:787; Z:22. III:13, 582B; P:VI, 193–94; T:1044; Z:275.

150. *In the early . . . to oneself.* I:39, 465A and *passim;* P:II, 142; T:244; Z:213. See above, pp. 41, 109.

150. *The problem is . . . useful to many.* III:9, 338B; P:VI, 17; T:922; Z:157. Cf. III:9, 414–20BC; P:VI, 73–78; T:962–65; Z:195–98. III:1 and III:10, *passim.*

150. *His real reason . . . in public office.* III:1, *passim.* For Montaigne's father, see III:10, 442–43B; P:VI, 93; T:975–76; Z:209.

150–51. *Public life must . . . by a miracle.* III:9, 414–16BC; P:VI, 73–74; T:962–63; Z:195–96.

151. *In other words . . . own dirty work.* III:9, 416–20BC; P:VI, 75–78; T:963–65; Z:196–98. Cf. III:1, *passim.*

151–52. *"Husbanding Your Will" . . . unnatural course.* III:10, 439–45BC; P:VI, 90–95; T:974–77; Z:207–10.

152. *The ideal balance . . . self-possessed loyalty.* III:1, 13–14B; P:V, 10–11; T:767; Z:3. Cf. III:10, *passim.*

152. *Proper self-possession . . . of our happiness.* III:10, 444B and *passim;* P:VI, 94; T:976–77; Z:210.

153. *Moreover, the incentive . . . and more legitimate.* III:2, 48–49BC; P:V, 34–35; T:783–84; Z:18–19.

153–54. *We are great fools . . . live appropriately.* III:13, 651C; P:VI, 243–44; T:1079; Z:309.

154. *We belong in nature . . . and so surely.* III:12, 531–32B; P:VI, 156–57; T:1019; Z:251.

154. *Nature helps us . . . follow her the better.* See II:12, 277–78A; P:III, 201; T:452; Z:130. III:4, 104B; P:V, 73; T:809; Z:44. III:10, 449–50B; P:VI, 98–99; T:979–80; Z:212–13. III:12 and III:13, *passim.*

154. *Artificiality is . . . glister for gold.* III:12, 506–7BC; P:VI, 138–39; T:1006–7; Z:238.

154. *Sometimes—and . . . a moment's notice.* III:12, 531–43BC; P:VI, 156–65; T:1019–25; Z:251–56.

154–55. *From the refusal . . . vice of hypocrisy.* III:2, 51–52B; P:V, 37; T:785; Z:20–21. III:3, 71B and note, and *passim;* P:V, 50; T:794 and note; Z:29 and note. III:5, 192–94BC and *passim;* P:V, 136–38; T:852–53; Z:87–88. III:9, 410–14BC; P:VI, 70–73; T:960–62; Z:193–95. III:13, 656B; P:VI, 247; T:1082; Z:311.

155. *Between ourselves . . . it is like inside.* III:13, 665–67BC; P:VI, 254–55; T:1087–88; Z:316. Cf. III:2, 42C; P:V, 30; T:781; Z:16.

155–56. *For self-study . . . condition of goodness.* III:12, 507–10B, 538B; P:VI, 139–41, 162; T:1007–8, 1022; Z:238–40, 254.

157. *I have not corrected . . . I combat nothing.* III:12, 552B; P:VI, 172; T:1029; Z:260.

157. *What virtue he . . . as he could.* II:11, 190A, 193A; P:III, 137, 139; T:408, 410; Z:86–88.

157. *Without boorish . . . forming his life.* II:37, 902A; P:IV, 264; T:762; Z:433.

157. *What they did . . . disposition (complexion).* III:10, 471–72B; P:VI, 114; T:991; Z:223.

157. *Habit is . . . than the first.* III:10, 450–51B; P:VI, 99; T:980; Z:213.

157. *Virtue can work . . . almost anything.* II:29, 742–43AC; P:IV, 149–50; T:684–85; Z:359–60.

158. *Reason will normally . . . we must follow.* II:8, 111A; P:III, 80; T:368; Z:50; see above, p. 100. Cf. II:37, 863A; P:IV, 236; T:742; Z:415. III:1, 18B; P:V, 14; T:770; Z:5.

158. *Shall I say this . . . devoutness and conscience.* III:12, 552C; P:VI, 172; T:1030; Z:260–61.

159. *Our vices . . . with inhumanity.* The references, in the order of listing, are these: III:3, 74C; P:V, 52; T:795; Z:30. III:13, 647B; P:VI, 241; T:1077; Z:307. III:9, 390–91B; P:VI, 55–56; T:949; Z:183. II:17, 631C; P:IV, 69; T:634; Z:311. III:9, 346B; P:VI, 23; T:926; Z:161. I:24, 246B; P:I, 182 (wrongly marked A); T:143; Z:113. II:5, 76C; P:III, 56–57; T:352; Z:34–35. III:6, 254B; P:V, 182; T:883; Z:119.

159. *the most solid . . . the most our own.* III:13, 662B; P:VI, 251; T:1085 (wrongly marked C); Z:314.

159. *An honorable man . . . all is human.* II:17, 631C; P:IV, 69; T:634; Z:311.

159. *Epaminondas . . . goodness and humanity.* III:1, 33B; P:V, 24–25; T:777; Z:12.

159. *Even for a god . . . more than human.* III:5, 162B; P:V, 115; T:837–38; Z:73.

159. *The most beautiful . . . well and duly.* III:13, 656B, 667BC; P:VI, 247, 255; T:1082, 1088; Z:311, 317.

160. *I hate that . . . as in age.* III:2, 61–62BC and *passim;* P:V, 43–44; T:789–90; Z:25.

160. *Now that his . . . to stay green.* III:5, 120B; P:V, 84; T:816; Z:51–52. Cf. III:5, 115–22B; P:V, 80–86; T:813–18; Z:49–53.

160. *The fairest souls . . . and a gardener.* III:3, 68B, 73B; P:V, 48, 52; T:792, 795; Z:27, 30. III:13, 599B; P:VI, 206; T:1053; Z:283–84.

160–61. *Praise of this . . . all sorts of perfection.* III:13, 650–55BC; P:VI, 243–46; T:1079–81; Z:308–11.

161. *It is an absolute . . . (loyallement).* III:13, 666B; P:VI, 255; T:1088; Z:316.

161. *Our well-being . . . always to follow.* II:12, 320A, 321C; P:III, 233–35; T:474–75; Z:152–53.

161. *This is the second . . . pleasure and pain.* II:15, *passim;* II:20, *passim;* II:37, 857–58A; P:IV, 232; T:739; Z:412.

161–62. *Our life is . . . than the other.* III:13, 612–13B; P:VI, 216; T:1060; Z:290.

162. *Naturally, we . . . through our fingers.* III:13, 656–59BC; P:VI, 247–49; T:1082–84; Z:311–13.

162. *If I had to . . . it is naturally.* III:2, 63C; P:V, 45; T:791; Z:26.

163. *As for me, then . . . all things good.* III:13, 661BC; P:VI, 250–51; T:1084–85; Z:313–14.

163. *Viresque acquirit eundo.* Virgil *Aeneid* IV. 175. See above, p. 139.

CONCLUSION

164. *Even as late . . . a gentilhomme . . .* I:26, 324A; P:II, 41; T:179; Z:149.

165. *almost all unfavorable . . . in the late.* There are only a few exceptions. Montaigne does note from the first that common people are often brave (I:23, 213A; P:I, 158; T:127; Z:98. I:54, 596–97A; P:II, 239; T:304; Z:274. II:7, 103A; P:III, 75; T:365; Z:47) and good (II:35, 823A; P:IV, 208; T:723; Z:397); that God chose his witnesses from among them (II:12, 333A; P:III, 244; T:482; Z:159); and that common sense, Montaigne's only distinction, is "vulgar, common, and plebeian" (II:17, 649A; P:IV, 83; T:643; Z:319). In his late years he still notes that they are ignorant and easily led (I:26, 281C; P:II, 11; T:159; Z:128. II:16, 583–84BC; P:IV, 36; T:610–11; Z:288–89. III:10, 458C; P:VI, 104; T:984; Z:216. III:13, 655B; P:VI, 246; T:1082; Z:311) and more afraid of pain than he (III:9, 334C; P:VI, 14; T:920; Z:154–55. III:13, 615B; P:VI, 218; T:1061; Z:291–92). Most of these are opinions that he expressed both early and late.

165. *He calls their conduct base and vile.* I:25, 255A; P:I, 188; T:146; Z:116.

165. *He contrasts them . . . excellent minds.* I:27, 343–47A; P:II, 55–58; T:188–91; Z:157–59. I:31, 389A; P:II, 88; T:210; Z:179. I:51,

584A; P:II, 229; T:299; Z:268. II:12, 246A, 324A; P:III, 177, 237; T:435–36, 476–77; Z:113, 154. II:37, 852A; P:IV, 229; T:736; Z:410.

165. *He finds "more . . . entirely on others".* I:42, 498–99A; P:II, 166; T:259; Z:229. It is worth noting that in his final version Montaigne suppressed several of these amenities: "ignorant," "asleep," "full of feverishness and fright."

165. *If we disdain . . . with these people.* III:3, 71BC; P:V, 50; T:794; Z:29.

165. *Socrates drew . . . cultivate it.* III:12, 506B, 508B, 531B, 537–38B; P:VI, 138, 140, 157, 161–62; T:1006–7, 1019, 1022; Z:238–39, 251, 254.

166. *He is "of the . . . consider myself".* II:17, 606C; P:IV, 51; T:621; Z:298. Cf. III:11, 498B; P:VI, 133; T:1003; Z:235.

166. *His life is . . . low and humble.* III:2, 40B; P:V, 29; T:779; Z:15. III:10, 463B; P:VI, 107; T:986; Z:219. III:13, 586B, 649C, 662B; P:VI, 196, 242, 251; T:1046, 1078, 1085 (wrongly marked C); Z:277, 308, 314.

166. *Whoever cannot . . . stupidity of mine.* III:10, 471B; P:VI, 114; T:991; Z:223.

166. *The best example . . . of the common herd.* II:12, 213A note, 475C; P:III, 152 (no note), 353; T:418 and note, 557; Z:96 and note (519), 234. Cf. DB:II, 18.

166–67. *He uses this term . . . of the courtier.* I:54, 598C; P:II, 240; T:305; Z:275. III:3, 79B; P:V, 56; T:797–98; Z:33. III:9, 362B, 394B, 404B, 405B; P:VI, 35, 58, 66; T:935, 951, 957; Z:169, 185, 190. III:13, 600B; P:VI, 206; T:1053; Z:283.

167. *The ideal of . . . enjoyed and admired.* See especially M. Magendie, *La Politesse mondaine et les théories de l'honnêteté, en France, au XVIIe siècle, de 1600 à 1660* (2 vols.; Alcan, n. d. [1926]), I, 387–93; II, 791; and *passim*. Also Boase, *The Fortunes of Montaigne*, pp. 295–410 and *passim;* René Pintard, *Le Libertinage érudit dans la première moitié du XVIIe siècle* (2 vols.; Boivin, 1943), *passim*.

167–68. *If the ideal . . . he should live.* Fortunat Strowski, *La Sagesse française* (Plon, n. d. [1925]), pp. 31–32, 44–45, 50–51, 96, 105, and *passim*. See also Joachim Merlant, *De Montaigne à Vauvenargues* (Société Française d'Imprimerie et de Librairie, 1914), pp. 1–87 and *passim*.

www.ingramcontent.com/pod-product-compliance
Lightning Source LLC
Chambersburg PA
CBHW070615310726
48982CB00001B/94
9780313241208